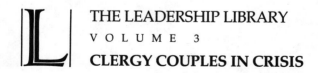

THE LEADERSHIP LIBRARY
V O L U M E 3
CLERGY COUPLES IN CRISIS

Other books in the Leadership Library

Well-Intentioned Dragons by Marshall Shelley

Liberating the Leader's Prayer Life by Terry Muck

THE LEADERSHIP LIBRARY

Volume

3

Clergy Couples in Crisis

The Impact of Stress on Pastoral Marriages

Dean Merrill

Carol Stream, Illinois

WORD BOOKS
PUBLISHER
WACO, TEXAS

A DIVISION OF
WORD, INCORPORATED

CLERGY COUPLES IN CRISIS

Copyright © 1985 by Christianity Today, Inc.

A LEADERSHIP/Word Book. Copublished by Christianity Today, Inc. and Word, Inc. Distributed by Word Books.

Cover art by Joe Van Severen

Unless otherwise marked, all Scripture quotations are from the New International Version of the Bible, © 1978 New York International Bible Society.

Library of Congress Cataloging in Publication Data

Merrill, Dean
Clergy couples in crisis

(The Leadership library; v. 3)
1. Clergy—Divorce. I. Title. II. Series
BV4395.5.M46 1985 248.8′92 85-47933
ISBN 0-917463-06-4

Printed in the United States of America

CONTENTS

ONE

THE ROCKETS'
RED GLARE

The maple trees that rimmed the church parking lot had almost finished their shedding that gray Tuesday morning as Martin Watson awaited his visitor. The *Washington Post* lay untouched on the coffee table of his study, between the right-angle couches where he counseled. The pastor had not had time to read the paper that morning; he was too busy going through files and wondering what the IRS agent had in mind.

The new wing of the church had been finished for a couple of years now, providing sorely needed classroom space. Watson had come to this suburban church in Fairfax, Virginia, more than a decade before. The congregation of two hundred that welcomed him was now closer to six hundred, and the trim, fifty-year-old pastor with graying hair had reason to be gratified. His two daughters were doing well in college, and he and Eva had been moved into a new parsonage not long ago.

The stranger with a briefcase arrived promptly at ten. He was cordial enough as he shook Martin's hand, then sat down across the desk. He delivered his message quietly: the Internal Revenue Service, as part of its ongoing program of review and enforcement, would be auditing the Watsons' last three years of tax returns. Martin pressed him for what might have triggered this inquiry, but the agent was noncommittal. He assured the pastor that the probe might turn up nothing at all— in fact, he hoped so.

The two men continued talking for a while, the pastor producing what records he had on hand and starting to jot a list of things to be collected for the next meeting.

There was a soft knock at the door.

"Come in," Martin called. His secretary entered. She hesitated as she looked at the agent, then handed her boss a Special Delivery envelope and quickly left.

Marvin looked at the sender's name. Some attorney he had never heard of in Alexandria.

"Excuse me a moment," he murmured to his visitor, who nodded.

He pulled a letter opener from his desk and sliced open the envelope. In a moment, he began reading:

Dear Rev. Watson:

This is to inform you that on Monday, November 13, a suit was filed in circuit court on behalf of Eva Watson to provide necessary funds for separate maintenance. . . .

He blinked twice. His breath seemed to stop. He could not hear the typewriters clicking in the outer office, nor the traffic outside, nor anything else. The only sound was within him— his heart, suddenly pounding at more than 120 beats a minute, it seemed.

I was absolutely stunned. I had no idea at that point, even though things had been rough, that she was actually going to . . . I couldn't say a word.

I just handed the letter to the agent.

He read it and took a deep breath. Finally he said, "Rev. Watson—you have enough problems. I'll see you in the spring." And he closed up his briefcase and left.

The actual separation came eight weeks later, on a Sunday night after a lavish farewell reception in the fellowship hall.

The congregation would not find out the facts until later; only the elders had been informed. They grieved in silence over the demise of this otherwise successful pastorate. When the appreciation speeches had ended and the long receiving line had finally been finished, Martin drove in the chilly darkness to an apartment he had rented across the Potomac in "the District." Eva spent the night with the board chairman and his wife. The next week she headed for her sister's in Annapolis.

Divorce—unthinkable in the Watsons' denomination, especially at the time this occurred in the early sixties—would not come for another nine years. Finally, all hope of reconciliation flickered out, and the stress of haranguing about money had exhausted them both. A lump-sum settlement was negotiated, and the Watson marriage—thirty-seven years running at that point—was finally buried.

The Greatest Fear

Among the hundreds of pastors LEADERSHIP editors meet, interview, or correspond with each year, the specter of a marital meltdown is usually their greatest fear. No other tragedy in the ministry holds such a threat. Virtually every month seems to include news of more personal pain, aborted pastorates, alienated offspring, and individuals called of God now trying to get through the long days and longer nights doing something else for a living.

In most other professions, the collapse of a marriage is now accommodated. Doctors, lawyers, educators, executives—such a thing in their lives causes hardly a murmur. No scorn is heaped upon the politician who must take time out for a divorce court hearing; indeed, he is rather the object of constituents' concern and empathy. In 1980 Americans elected their first divorced President, and returned him with a landslide in 1984. A major bloc of his coalition: conservative Christians.

But when it comes to pastors . . . the stakes remain high.

Some denominations still automatically defrock a divorcing

pastor; others require an unpaid sabbatical of varying lengths. In still others, the leadership may be willing to aid, counsel, and eventually guide the divorced minister toward another parish, but local congregations remain wary. If a church does vote to accept such a pastor, the official act is only part of the battle; the trust and respect of individuals must still be won, often over a long time and at great cost.

If the minister decides to step out of the denomination and take (or form) an independent church, he often finds himself a reluctant magnet for others with irregular pasts, both clergy and laypeople. Those with intact marriages seem harder to attract.

The demise of a pastoral marriage—in addition to its bone-deep personal pain, which every divorcing couple experiences—carries immense professional consequences. Thus pastors know they simply *must* make their marriages work, or suffer a double aftermath.

The concern crosses all age groups. Marital crises do not happen only to the young and foolish. In fact, can any reader look back on the last twelve months and *not* recall a moment— a telephone call, a quiet sentence from a friend, perhaps a written notice—that produced a sinking sensation: another ministry marriage had collapsed? As one district superintendent said recently, not in jest but in despair, "Don't even talk to me about pastoral marriages. I've heard so much the past few months I can't take anymore."

It is almost as if we are standing on the ramparts with Francis Scott Key, watching the nighttime sky turn luminous with the rockets' red glare, one after another hurtling through space and plunging to a fiery end. The concussions reverberate through congregations and districts—not to mention those whose lives take a direct hit and can never be rebuilt. No denomination or fellowship appears exempt. The bombardment rages on; it is an evil time.

The purpose of this book, therefore, is disarmament. It is to show where the explosives lie and how they may be defused.

Much of the attention here is given to the stories of current pastoral couples. To read of the dangers they have faced and how they have coped—or failed to cope—is to see pieces of our own lives. The accounts that follow have been gathered from in-depth interviews, usually over a two-day period, with nearly twenty carefully selected ministry couples. Husbands and wives were interviewed together and also separately, one spouse at a time. In order to allow them to speak freely, they were assured that all references in the book would be camouflaged.

What that means is that the names of persons, towns, churches, and denominations have been changed, along with any other "giveaway" identifications. What has *not* been changed is the essence of their experience. All direct quotations are accurate, nearly verbatim from the tape recorder and edited only for clarity and conciseness. The accounts here are thus the *equivalent* of what really happened—neither rosier nor more grim. They are documentary accounts of real-life experience with only enough alteration to prevent tracing.

Following each account comes a reflection by a well-qualified Christian author and counselor of clergy couples. Drs. Gary Collins, Louis McBurney, and David Seamands bring their expertise to bear upon the cases recorded here and make insightful observations for the benefit of all. They do so in hopes of preventing the tragedy and long-term loneliness such as the Watsons endure.

Living with the Pain

Today, Martin Watson lives quietly in the basement apartment of a friend, spending his days tending flowers and walking in the neighborhood—up to forty blocks some days, since a heart attack several years ago.

His grandfatherly bearing belies the pain of his past—the late-night arguments, the gradual distance within the marriage, the fading of romance, the loss of respect, and the struggle to keep preaching and praying and administrating all the while. There is no One Great Cause to uncover here—no affair, no rebellion against the faith or even the ministry. There is only an ever-darkening trail of tension, conflict, and finally tears.

And the end was not the end. When a marriage detonates, as any divorced person will tell you, the debris lives on; it is not biodegradable. The spouses simply cannot pretend it's a new world and the other partner has left for Saturn. Children, money, holidays, memories, and a dozen other things keep raising their hands for attention.

In the early months, the Watsons met more than once to talk about reunion but always stalemated. Meanwhile, in order to try to meet support payments, Martin first took a job managing a car leasing office. Within weeks his boss, an earthy man, said, "You know, you can't even tell a *white* lie. You really need to do something else." Next came life insurance, then fund raising, and finally a position with a county hospital. Now, in retirement, he still makes visits there two days a week.

He turns to his interviewer and says:

> I want you to know I don't think I've done everything right in my life. But I don't know how I could have told it to you any differently and still told how I felt. . . . As I hash this over, it really sounds awful, and I'm making her out almost to be an ogre. There was another side of her that could be generous.
>
> I think a death is easier than a divorce, because there's a finality to it. This sort of thing—it goes on. It still isn't over for me, even though I'm not half as resentful now as I was.
>
> In spite of everything—I think about her getting older by herself. She has several good friends there in the church. But I just wish it had never been. Some things, I guess, are not reversible.

Eva Watson, seventy-five, lives alone in a second-floor flat in Trenton, New Jersey, and still holds a job as a clinic receptionist. She retains a hearty laugh at times. She speaks her mind when the subject turns to Martin, frequently wandering into side stories about old friends, but sooner or later returning to make her point.

She bears the wary visage of a divorcee, the textured skin around the eyes that says, *I've been through a lot.* She makes sure her visits to her daughters do not coincide with Martin's, even at Christmastime.

It's too frustrating and upsetting to me. Betty will be in the midst of cooking or whatever, and he'll want all these things to be done for him. Always needing someone to cater.

He just never thinks of the other person. It was that way from the very beginning.

Is there anything *she* would like to go back and do differently? The question puzzles her; she honestly cannot think of a reply, except that maybe she shouldn't have criticized his table manners so much. What has she learned through this whole ordeal? Only "that I was a chump—too naive. I took him at face value, and I shouldn't have."

When were the best times? When was her husband *least* self-centered, in her view? Again, she draws a blank.

What is perhaps most tragic is that twenty-one years after separation, so little has mellowed. The accusations remain as astringent as ever, the stories as one-sided (and therefore contradictory) as they must have been two decades ago. There still is not resolution and acceptance. Both continue church attendance and profess a love and commitment to God. But reconciliation or even reinterpretation of the facts is apparently too much to hope for.

Such a case fills us with sadness—but also reminds us that while the flaws in other marriages are often clear to us, we cannot afford to be smug about our own. As every pastoral counselor knows, prevention is a far better exercise than cure. The following pages focus first on the stresses of the early years in ministry, then on those problems that arise out of congregational life, and finally on the personal pressures that would put asunder what God hath joined together and ordained to his work.

Part One
BEGINNINGS

"I read recently that 80 percent of seminarians come from large churches, and yet 80 percent of the churches are small," says Alban Institute consultant Roy Oswald. He calls that "a cross-cultural barrier as tough as any foreign mission field."

In fact, he goes so far as to say "the difference between seminary religion and parish religion is greater than the difference between denominations."[1] In other words, it is easier to grow up Baptist and switch to Methodism than to move from a seminary to the pastorate of one of its supporting churches.

Most pastoral couples know exactly what he is talking about. They remember the heady intellectualism of seminary life, the animated conversations with classmates about how to reform Christendom, the dreams of future honor and achievement in the parish. Then came reality.

The transition is softened somewhat when a couple starts on a large-church staff. Expectations often run lower and are less focused. To become the one and only pastor of a small church, on the other hand, is to face major adjustment.

Thankfully, most young pastoral couples have a secret defense: flexibility. They can stand anything for a while. There's always tomorrow. Don't all professionals have to start at the bottom and work their way up? This too shall pass.

One couple remembers serving a congregation so nasty that "it wasn't actually a church; it was a group of mean people who got together on Sunday mornings," says the husband. "I finally ran an experiment: I preached on hell and judgment three Sundays in a row, just to see what would happen. At the door an elder commented, 'Finally learnin' how to preach, son.' "

What made this whole ordeal bearable was that this was a student pastorate—simply a way to pay the bills during seminary. "We had great family life during those years. Our favorite time of the week was Friday night, when we'd sprawl on the floor with our three little kids and watch 'Planet of the Apes.' "

Such memories make for lively reminiscing at ministerial coffee breaks now. The hard times of early days are tossed off with a chuckle.

But for others, the first-church experience is no laughing matter.

They came expecting to make allowances, of course. They knew they would have to get along with a board. They were prepared to be watched. They had some notion that there would be cherished traditions in this congregation. What they were, of course, remained to be discovered.

But the pressure turned out to be far greater than imagined. More than one wife has found her behavior suddenly subjected to a new and unfamiliar grid: How will this reflect on the ministry? She has not been accustomed to evaluating every move, every word, for its public relations impact. Her husband, however, may have unconsciously posted a dictum over the home straight from 1 Corinthians 10:32–33: "Give none offence, neither to the Jews, nor to the Gentiles, nor to the church of God: Even as I please all men in all things."

In other cases, both husband and wife find themselves in culture shock. They can hardly think of doing anything as leaders in the ministry; they are too consumed with their new state of being. Yet ministers are supposed to be pro-active. How?

The following case studies show couples who have survived these threats to pastoral marriage. The "Reflections" sections are provided by Dr. Gary Collins, psychologist, author, and professor at Trinity Evangelical Divinity School, Deerfield, Illinois.

1. Roy Oswald, "The Pastor's Passages," LEADERSHIP, Fall 1983, pp. 18-19.

The Franciscos:
FACES IN THE NIGHT

Jeff and Linda Francisco brought more than fourteen years of higher education to the shady streets and quiet sidewalks of Hooper, Nebraska, a farm town fifty miles northwest of Omaha. Jeff, a native of Boston, had begun working with Inter-Varsity Christian Fellowship while in seminary, helping dorm Bible studies get going at Harvard and M.I.T. and guiding students toward an adult-level faith. Linda was a well-trained minister of music at a Cambridge church who was continuing her studies at a conservatory. They were both twenty-six years old when they married.

Campus ministry with a parachurch organization was exciting but hectic, and there was always the pressure to keep one eye on fund raising. Linda taught high school to help make ends meet, but after Jennifer was born, she could only substitute. Jeff began to think about how he actually enjoyed preaching, and when his denomination invited parachurch workers such as himself to prepare for ordination via a fast-track seminary program, he signed up. Within six months, the Franciscos were on their way to Hooper—"a good, solid church," said the bishop.

They moved in the dead of winter. The first Sunday went

well enough, although as Jeff looked around at the eighty worshipers, he realized young faces were few and far between, and he would have to learn to communicate more with grandpas and grandmas.

Following his natural instincts, however, he issued an invitation for the confirmation class (all four of them) to come for dinner the next Friday evening.

That Tuesday morning, Linda had her first caller. Boxes were still piled high in the parsonage dining room, and the new pastor's wife was in jeans preparing to tackle the mountain. Jennifer had just gone down for her nap when the doorbell rang.

It was the wife of the church chairman.

> She was the kind of person who gave you the distinct impression she wanted you to know her life was all put together very well.
>
> She sat down and wanted to know if I would have tea and cookies with her.
>
> I said, "Well, I can find some tea; I don't know about the cookies!" Her son was one of the confirmation kids who'd be coming three days later. I said, "I'm glad you're here; do you mind wandering around with me while I try to find my way through this confusion here? I need to get some things unpacked."
>
> And she said, well yes, she did mind. She would rather sit down, and could we have tea together at the table?

Linda gulped and began clearing off a space. The woman soon made it clear that she didn't think much of mugs, and so the search began for legitimate cups.

> I sat down thinking, *Oh—so much to do!* We talked for a little while. And then she looked me right in the eye and said in a breathy tone, "Linda—how are you doing?"
>
> I gasped. I felt suddenly just a little naked in front of her. I don't remember what I finally said, but I must have made light of her comment; I didn't know what she was expecting from me.

That was a fatal mistake. It was soon followed by another, when Linda finished her tea and then said, "I've really enjoyed talking with you, but if you don't mind—I have so much to do. The baby will be waking up soon, and you're welcome to stay and chat here while I just sort of wander back and forth. . . ." The woman quickly excused herself.

By the next weekend, Jeff was hearing through the congregation about how ungracious his haughty wife had been. He came home to demand, "What in the world did you say to her?!" Linda was doubly shattered—not only that the woman had slandered her but that Jeff had not immediately trusted and defended her.

She told herself she would need to be far more careful from now on. Was this really what every pastor's wife went through?

By the next month, Linda was again pregnant. She began to be homesick for Boston. A blizzard raged across the prairie, and then another one; people darted from their homes to the post office to the grocery store and back inside again, hardly speaking. Linda felt depression and anxiety beginning to set in.

She mentioned it to Jeff one night. He brushed it aside by saying, "I'm sure you'll be better when spring comes and after the baby's born."

Linda met one woman in the church about her age who became a prayer partner. A measure of trust developed. One week as they met, Linda pulled back the curtain of her life just a bit. "I'm having a hard time these days. I really feel kind of . . . well, it's hard to describe. Some nights I'm not sleeping. I think I need to get some help. Would you pray for me? What do you think I should do?"

The woman visibly recoiled, as if to say, *You didn't really want to tell me this, did you?* She could not make her exit fast enough. Her own marriage, in fact, was disintegrating, but she could only allude to the problem, not discuss it.

This reinforced Linda's aloneness.

I was always put on a pedestal at church. In a superficial sense I was very much loved and doted upon—my birthday was over-celebrated, for example. It was almost like a compensation going on.

Meanwhile, people were aching and bleeding all over that church. But nobody would deal with it.

The loneliness deepened, the crying, the headaches. Linda began to think about all the Inter-Varsity friends she missed. She kept brooding all that summer, facing each day with a tight lip.

A quiet desperation was brewing inside, part of it aimed at Jeff: *Why doesn't he hurt the way I do?* She wanted him to understand her feelings. But at the same time, she didn't want him to fall under the weight; she wanted him to remain strong so she could lean on him.

Jeremy was born in November, and she was temporarily happy about giving her husband a son. But within weeks, the roiling clouds of depression returned. She had no hint of the voltage building up in their gray masses.

A pastors' conference came to Omaha in February. Jeff registered to attend, and when he realized a number of old friends would be there as well, he urged Linda to find a baby sitter for one day.

It was a marvelous splurge of renewing old acquaintances. After every session, another familiar face would materialize in the corridors to exclaim, "Hi! How *are* you?" Conversation would fly at breakneck speed for the next ten minutes, trying to cover years of absence. Then there would be someone else—another session—someone else—someone else, from morning to night.

It was exciting. Jeff and Linda drove back to Hooper that night exhilarated. They thanked the woman who had cared for their two children all day and then fell into bed exhausted.

Sometime after midnight, the nightmares began. Faces . . .

old friends, fading in and out of Linda's view . . . young associates from Boston . . . members of the church . . . coming toward her, moving off to the right, the left . . . leaving her alone.

> All of a sudden, I started hallucinating. I can't quite describe what happened. There were lights and visions, and I started crying and screaming. I sat bolt upright in bed, and Jeff did too. I was trembling and sobbing. I tried to tell him, "Everybody's leaving me! No one's staying around." Even Jeff had been so busy with the church. I remember thinking, *The only people in the world who don't fade in and out of my life are my two kids. . . . There's no permanence to any relationship I know.*

Jeff clung to his wife and tried to calm her. The trembling and sobbing subsided after a while. Then she grew more agitated again, as a new thought struck her brain: *I bet I'm so bad they're going to take me away from my children because I'm an unfit mother!* The two little people who in some ways oppressed Linda with their many needs, yet were so dependent upon her and were at least reliable to be there—*what if I lose them, too?* She became hysterical, pleading with Jeff, "Don't let them take the children away!"

Jeff pulled her close and simply said, "I will stay right here and hold you until morning."

Linda says now, "That was probably something I had needed for months—just to be held. Not as a prelude to anything else, but just because. . . ."

When the sun came up across the frozen fields, Jeff quickly got on the phone to a doctor. Linda was given a physical examination that day and then a 100-question test to measure stress build-up. When the nurse brought in the results, the doctor's eyes grew large as he tried to hold his composure. Finally he said, "We assume that anyone who accumulates 350 points will have trouble making it through the day. . . . You have 720 points." He began asking if Linda had contemplated suicide. She confessed she had but said the children kept her from it.

Linda was sent home with an antidepressant, some tranquilizers, and an appointment to begin seeing a psychiatrist. Every day for the next week, the medical doctor called to see how she was doing. The drugs began to take effect, and she calmed down.

Her only new worry was what if the church found out what had happened. That embarrassment was dealt with, however.

Jeff and I decided we wouldn't make major announcements, but in the course of being who we were, we'd let people know what was happening with us. Even if some looked askance, we needed to do this, because I couldn't go on living a façade anymore.

Several people responded sympathetically to that, while others were very frightened by it, and others pretended they didn't know. But for me, it was very good.

Linda went through two series of therapy, the first to get her through the immediate crisis and teach her how to care for her own mental health. Jeff went along to the appointments, to learn what he could as well. The psychiatrist held them accountable for things like dates together and even getting to bed on time so they would not be irritable the next day. Jeff came to understand more about his wife's emotional disposition and how insensitive he had been to her needs. He says:

As you can tell, Linda is more forceful, one who deals with a situation. I'm more laid back and think most things will resolve themselves without my effort. She's more dominant in pushing for resolution, wanting to see how the pieces will fit together.

I guess I keep referring to a confidence in God, that he's going to give us wisdom and help us put things together, and I don't have to see everything in black and white. Maybe I do that too much.

They learned that Jeff's natural desire to be a pacifier had been short-circuiting some needed confrontations. The counselor explained that when a basic commitment exists between a husband and wife, it gives the latitude to slug it out, to wrestle with the issues. "You have a greater freedom to confront and resolve things because you are secure; you *know* the other person is not going to turn on his heel and walk out the door. This is a great asset; use it," he said.

One issue to be aired was leisure time. Jeff, while working hard in a difficult church, could always stop by the YMCA in the next town for a workout while doing business there or making hospital calls. It was a healthy outlet for his body and mind. Linda resented that—and then scorned herself for objecting; after all, her husband needed the exercise. But when was *her* turn?

Jeff would say, "Well, I'll come home from the church early one afternoon a week, and you go run." The idea of running at four-thirty in the afternoon left her cold.

Time for more talk, more accommodation, more understanding.

By the time Linda had been in therapy for a year, she was feeling much better about herself. She could cope with mothering, with the pace of life in Hooper, with the requirements of her role.

It was still very difficult for me to write; it was probably three years before I wrote a letter. An emotional paralysis would come over me whenever I sat down to write to someone who knew the real me. There was so much I wanted to say I didn't know where to start. I'd just dissolve in tears right over the paper.

But in time, Linda began to reach out to her world once again. A women's Bible study in the church developed more authenticity under her guidance. Although many women were threatened by its openness and dropped out, some remained—not only young mothers but one woman in her seventies as well, who became Linda's surrogate mother.

Near the end of their four years at this church, another daughter was born, and Linda remembers this as a happy time. She calls these years "a significant growing time for us. We learned to notice the signals of trouble. We learned to communicate about our needs before reaching a crisis point. We learned to hear one another."

REFLECTIONS
by Gary Collins

The early crisis in this ministry marriage is created in part by the education gap. The Franciscos are like many seminarians who graduate, go into a little community, and get immediately frustrated. Even students who say they're glad to get away from the books find this happening. It's a form of sensory deprivation.

Instead of books, they find people like this chairman's wife, who come bounding by the parsonage for visits at inopportune moments. Or the pastor goes to his study, and the sight of his car outside the church becomes an invitation for drop-ins. (We seminary professors didn't talk much about these kinds of problems.)

It seems that whenever I talk to pastors, no matter how well prepared they are for the ministry, I hear about situations in which somebody in the church is unhappy. You simply can't please all the people all the time. That presents problems if you're not expecting it, or if you've got nobody to talk to. Obviously, the best person to talk to is your spouse or another friend. For Linda Francisco, neither of these worked. Jeff said he thought things would be all right once the baby came, and the church chairman's wife showed her insensitivity right away. So Linda talked to another woman in the church, and as soon as the conversation began to open up, the friend got threatened and backed off.

Then came the pastors' conference. Everybody opened up there. They saw old friends and were reminded of all they'd been missing. As soon as they drove back to their small community, Linda was hit with a middle-of-the-night anxiety attack.

This raises the point of how we deal with frustrations. Men frequently cope by jumping into their work. Jeff, like most pastors, was a young dynamo, ready to go, enthusiastic. A former student of mine recently said, "One characteristic of many Yuppies is that they are very good at managing their careers but not the other parts of their lives." I think pastors are like that sometimes. They are better at managing the church than managing their families, their bodies, their time, or their spiritual lives. And we didn't prepare them in seminary. The only thing we taught them to manage was the Hebrew text.

I realize you cannot fully teach life management, but you can model it. You can also discuss it. You can alert people to the dangers. If the only models students see are academicians who read books, they will go out and try to be academicians who read books.

When a pastor, a pastor's spouse, or for that matter anyone else is frustrated, the standard psychological theory says this frustration almost always leads to aggression. So what do you do? Lash out at people? That's not very safe in the pastorate, because you'll be criticized. You learn to keep your mouth shut.

Sometimes we lash out with kind of a passive aggression—lack of cooperation, for example, or gossip. Church members do that. Pastoral people do, too.

More often we hold the anger inside. It sometimes comes out in psychosomatic illnesses, and sometimes it explodes, as in Linda's case. Sometimes it comes out in depression. Very often, depression is the result of anger held inside.

A veteran pastor said to me one day, "My wife has *always* been depressed." I suspect that is because she's always been angry. She apparently can't talk to anybody about her anger—her husband, a church member, or even another pastor's wife, because it would look like complaining. So she keeps it inside and wonders why she's depressed.

When Linda Francisco's crisis came, her husband did exactly the right thing. He reached out and said, "I'll hold you until the morning." There couldn't have been a better therapy.

Of course, she went to a professional counselor, but the real breakthrough was this: She got her husband's attention. I don't think she was deliberately trying to do that, but that was the result.

(Some of Linda's problem, it must be said, may simply have been postpartum depression. The birth of a child brings physical and hormonal changes that can contribute to depression and anxiety.)

Many men (me included) tend to withdraw into our work when we start seeing things shake a little at home. The kids start acting up, there's dissension, or somebody starts getting depressed— and we retreat. We go where it's safe, where we know what we're doing. We can be in control. It's fun. It's exciting. The worse the problems get, the more we deny them. We are busy "serving the Lord with gladness" while our families are falling apart.

Then suddenly the crisis breaks, and we have to face it.

It's tough for a wife to get angry at a husband who's serving the Lord. If he were working for IBM, it would be different. But to get mad at a *pastor* means you're indirectly getting mad at God. That puts guilt on you and more discouragement, so you keep it inside.

Gordon Allport, past president of the American Psychological Association and a professor at Harvard, once said the biggest problem with pastors in this country is that they have no interpersonal skills. That's a harsh statement, I realize, but he's not completely wrong. Pastors, if they are not careful, can relate to books and theological ideas far better than they relate to people. And the hardest place to relate to people is at home.

Jeff Francisco, besides being insensitive in the beginning, was also insecure. After all, this was his first church, and the chairman's wife was already unhappy. All rookie pastors feel a certain amount of insecurity. When we get older, we already know we can succeed; if we fail, we pick up and go on. But you certainly don't want to fail in the first round. So you're very alert to criticism. All that keeps you from seeing what's going on at home.

Today, the Franciscos remember that "people were aching and bleeding all over that church. But nobody would deal with it." It's hard to admit personal struggle, because many people think it goes against Christian theology. We're supposed to have it all together, rejoice, be bubbling over and victorious.

It is *especially* hard to admit the pastor or the pastor's wife isn't victorious. The more common alternative is denial, quiet desperation, hiding in busyness.

Regarding the doctor who gave her a hundred-question test: Perhaps it should be said that psychological tests are often not as accurate as this implies. They give us clues, but many people seem to handle large numbers of "stress points" very well. Others have minimal stress and fall apart.

It was extremely important, however, that the doctor got her to admit thoughts of suicide. We have a suicide epidemic in this country, especially among young people. Many consider it the only way out. I can see how Linda came to this stage, feeling as she did that she had no husband to talk to, no friends to talk to, no way to get out of the environment, no place of freedom. She couldn't even exercise. At least her husband could do that.

The two little children further boxed her in. She began thinking, *I can't take this much longer*. At this point, counseling became crucial for her.

The Franciscos' decision about how to handle the news of psychotherapy was well done. They didn't make a major announcement, but neither did they try to hide it. In this they modeled something to the people in the congregation who were growing: A Christian doesn't have to have it all together, and it's OK to go for counseling.

The response is interesting: Some were sympathetic, some were scared, and some pretended they didn't know what was going on. That's about average for this kind of event! The sympathetic ones respond as they would to a death or other concern in the congregation. But others are threatened, and others don't know what to do so they don't do anything.

As I went through this narrative, I kept thinking about systems theory, which is a popular approach right now. It says the family is a system, and whenever one member is dysfunctional, he or she is *not* the only one with the problem. The whole family has the problem. (An example: Let's say a husband and wife don't get along. Their teenage son gets into drinking. Who's got the problem? They can send the kid for counseling, but he will have to go back to that same family situation that helped create the problem in the first place.) So we have to work with the entire family.

In the present case, Linda was the one having hallucinations and shaking in the night. But she was not the only one with a problem. A lot of times, one person will be crying for help, but the whole family is dysfunctional.

The fact that Jeff and Linda together tackled *their* problem was good. He went along to the counseling sessions. He found out what he was doing inadvertently to contribute to the problem.

She could have gone to counseling for years with no change if he hadn't changed.

I have discovered in my own life that I often have wonderful ways to solve my wife's problems. My solutions are nice and concise—except that she doesn't own them. Therefore, they don't necessarily work for her. I'm just like Jeff suggesting his wife go jogging at four-thirty in the afternoon. I have to learn to work *with* her on finding solutions.

Finally, it is interesting that it took Linda awhile to get over her paralysis about writing letters. When you get depressed, when you get really down, you don't snap out of it. Sometimes people come for counseling with the attitude "I'll go a couple of times and get things fixed." These problems took *years* to develop, and they're not going to evaporate in two sessions.

The beginning decade of adulthood may be one of the hardest times in life. It is a time to learn to be on your own, to set your values and lifestyle, to learn interpersonal skills, money management skills, time management skills. All this can be very difficult.

Once this couple mastered some of these skills and developed more self-confidence, they discovered they could be more open. The people in Linda's Bible study who were threatened dropped out, but others found it great. They could identify with her and, therefore, she began having a ministry.

Her final sentence says it all: "We learned to communicate about our needs before reaching a crisis point. We learned to hear one another." The sooner we face into a matter of tension, the easier it is to deal with it. The longer we let things go, the bigger the problem becomes. That is why many couples don't arrive at the happy ending this couple found.

THREE

The Owenses:
WHEN IN ROME . . .

When David Owens brought his city bride, Jacqueline, to a small Bible Baptist church in Bolivar, Tennessee, in the early 1960s, they followed a long succession of short pastorates. David, however, was enthusiastic about the potential in this town of seven thousand; he had grown up only fifty miles away and knew the area.

Unlike the Franciscos, there was not a major educational gap in this case. David was a Bible college graduate; Jackie, three years younger, had done no college at all. The young couple had traveled the previous summer, speaking and singing at youth camps and children's meetings; now they were looking forward to their own church.

David set a blistering pace at first, calling, studying, praying, fasting—doing everything he could to make this church grow. He visited the local lumber yard to ask the cost of excavating a basement under the little white church for more Sunday school space. He got his figure—and later on, a two-hour rebuke from the trustees for delving into something outside his area. He was there to preach, and that was all.

Meanwhile, Jackie was quickly realizing this was a long way from 4,400-member Houston Baptist Temple where she had grown up.

I was very much a free spirit—I guess I still am. I don't like being put into a mold. I want the satisfaction of saying, "This is what I am and how I act or don't act, because it's right or wrong." I want to make the choice—not have somebody tell me, "You'd better ____ because of who you are."

Her husband calls her a prankster and a daredevil—"vinegar and life to the extreme"—and loves her for it. They had met one summer when Jackie came to visit her uncle, who pastored David's home church. On several occasions during courtship they had locked horns over questions about makeup and clothing styles. David had been greatly relieved (even grateful for answered prayer, he said) when Jackie had agreed to rein in her flamboyance.

I saved some of his letters, and when our own daughters read them now, they just howl. "Dad, we can't *believe* you wrote this stuff to Mom!" David gets embarrassed at how legalistic he was. But at the time, it was very important to him. There was just no way his wife was going to sit in church with earrings and lipstick and nail polish on.

And I wanted to do the right thing. I didn't want to be a hindrance or a thorn. I may have been dying inside, but I thought, *If this is what I have to do to be a pastor's wife—this is what I have to do.* That was it. There was no choice.

Once in Bolivar, however, she continued to press the edges of acceptable fashion—a necklace here, a curled eyelash there. The heat began to build. It came partly from the congregation but even more from older pastors in the association—and particularly older pastors' wives. Jackie's hair was too short, her clothes too modern, her overall carriage too sexy.

"Why do you wear those pearls?" one woman asked at a ministerial gathering.

"Because I *like* them," Jackie shot back.

"But *why* do you like them?"

"Because when I'm getting dressed, I simply look in the mirror and think, *Oh, this string of pearls would look nice with this outfit.* I don't feel like I'm complete until I've added—"

"No, no, that's not the reason," the older woman said. "You wear them for sex appeal."

Jackie could not hold her tongue. "You're crazy!"

(Now, more than twenty years later, times have changed drastically. Most of her former critics now dress as stylishly as she does, and they laugh together about the early days.)

David had little time or inclination to think about such discussions; he was too busy trying to ignite this church. He also had to patch together a living somehow. The $35-a-week salary was simply not enough, and so he went to work as a farmhand outside of town, putting in up to sixty hours a week for a dollar an hour.

Their first daughter had been born before coming to Bolivar, and a second one arrived during the two years they were there.

Meanwhile, Jackie seethed . . . but conformed.

> In those years, all the motivation for ministry I'd had as a young girl left me. I was so totally wiped out as a person.
>
> They said I was ruining David. So I gave away every piece of jewelry I owned, even a beautiful jewelry box he had given me when we were going together.
>
> It wasn't good enough to throw the eyelash curler away, because I knew if I put it in the trash, I wouldn't be able to stand it, and the next day I'd go take it out again. So I put it on the floor and stepped on it—crushed it—knowing full well we could not afford to buy a new one.

David regrets to this day that he did not support his wife. "I guess I just encouraged her to knuckle under and be dowdy. See, I'd grown up in this kind of environment. Everything was negative, and the only way to see revival was to 'preach the clothesline' so people would get straightened out and God could bless . . . that was my whole mindset back then. I was terrible."

But neither his wife's comedown nor his fervent praying brought the breakthrough David sought. "I was buying Rolaids by the carton," he remembers. The congregation of thirty had grown only to forty-five by the time the Owenses were exhausted and ready to consider a new call. Two years after they left, the church closed its doors—but not before the pastor who followed them, an older man, had insisted that the board send David a letter of apology for its obstinance.

The next congregation—and its neighboring pastors—were not so legalistic about appearance. And of course, Jackie was more compliant by then. They stayed in Van Wert, Ohio, six years; here a baby son was born.

The pressure in this place, Jackie soon realized, was more social: much of it revolved around who would be best friend of the pastor's wife. The Owenses were also frequently criticized for not going to someone's house for Sunday dinner—even though no invitation had been extended. Parishioners would drive around town checking where the pastoral car was parked, and criticisms seemed to sprout like spring weeds.

Nevertheless, good things began to happen in the church along with the bad. Some doctrinal aberrations were corralled, and attendance climbed from 60 to 160, which filled the building.

The matter of David's workaholism was yet to be dealt with (see chapter 14). In fact, the combination of factors might have sunk Jackie for good had not a wise and attentive God steered David into an experiment as a traveling evangelist. Jackie retreated with the children to David's home town in Tennessee, where her parents-in-law could provide a rent-free house.

> Finally, I was no longer the pastor's wife. I jumped over the traces. I put color in my hair; I decided to wear some make-up; I wore what I wanted. I got active in the women's club in town, the PTA, women's Bible studies. . . .

When David would call each Sunday night, however, too often it was to say his week of preaching had netted only enough money to buy gasoline to the next stop. Jackie took to selling Avon door to door on a country route, dodging German shepherds in the farmers' yards. At the end of a day, she might pick up her spirits by taking her brood to a greasy spoon on the highway for hamburgers. When cabin fever struck, she would rearrange the furniture.

December came, and several churches canceled their bookings around the Christmas/New Year's holidays, so David returned home and sought temporary work. The only job he found was as a gravedigger.

> I was out there in the middle of winter with a pneumatic air machine—*d-d-d-d-d!*—breaking up the frost. It liked to killed me! But I'd been away from the family for three months straight, and at least I was home nights.
>
> I do *not* know how we made it. At the end of that year and three months, we were $2,500 in debt, *despite* having no house payment and no car payment all the while.
>
> The only benefit was that I got to travel and study a lot of different churches. I got to analyze what was working and what was not. It was an invaluable education for returning to the pastorate.

Today this couple leads a large church with a sizable staff in Phoenix, Arizona; their ministry has stabilized and prospered beyond any early imagination. They worry hardly at all these days about either fashions or money; Jackie is busy as a senior pastor's wife speaking, organizing, being a hostess, and enjoying her first grandchild. David is at his prime of effectiveness. They have taken a church of seventy-five and built it to a thousand over the last sixteen years, set free by a congregation more concerned about outreach and love than tradition and hemlines.

It is not unreasonable to say, with hindsight, that their break from the pastorate, even though only fifteen months long, was critically timed and in fact salvaged their future. Without it, they might have become casualties.

REFLECTIONS
by Gary Collins

Here is youthful idealism hitting the real world. Actually, it's good that people in their twenties and early thirties are willing to try things we older people wouldn't try. At least we get shaken out of our ruts that way.

They come out of school brimming with creative ideas for church growth. They go down to the lumber yard to find out about excavating the church basement—and everybody screams bloody murder. One suggestion, and their wrists get slapped. This is what makes life difficult for many new pastors.

It takes awhile to discover the wisdom of saying to the church board, "Here's an idea that maybe we could think about some-time." Nobody is threatened by that, but three or four months later somebody brings up the same suggestion and thinks it's theirs. That's all right; at least things get changed that way.

I once heard that changing a university is like trying to reorganize a cemetery. The same can probably be said of churches. This is very difficult for people who are eager to get going now that they don't have to write those dumb term papers anymore. David Owens went to the lumber yard thinking he was being efficient, getting things done, being a "mover"—but the church was threatened.

The problem for many of us is how to be creative and submissive at the same time! That's very hard. Anybody who works in an organization faces this. How can I be creative without making too many waves or knocking heads with my superiors?

A lot depends on being positive, willing to encourage people, and pointing out the good things they do. Then when we present new ideas, others don't feel threatened.

In our society, success and self-worth go together. If a church "fails," the young pastor doesn't say, *This was a bad situation* (even though in this case, the following pastor insisted the Bolivar board send an apology to the Owenses, and the congregation later folded). What the young pastor tells himself is, *The church is no good, and I'm tied to it; therefore I'm no good.*

This makes us struggle for success in order to boost our own self-worth. The Scriptures say we are all accepted in the eyes of

God because he loved us "even while we were yet sinners." But that's not the way our society operates. Society says if you fail, this reflects your worth. So you take it personally.

If you've had three successful pastorates in a row and then one bombs, you can handle it. But if you haven't had any successes to date, you don't know whether you're any good. You go on being controlled by "the tyranny of the urgent," to use Hummel's expression, putting out fires in the church and thinking you can tend to your spouse and family later.

Regarding the lipstick, earrings, and later on, wearing pearls: Male pastors must try hard to understand what is important to wives. We get busy and forget that women value many things differently than men do.

I always thought flowers were dumb. Why? Because they're expensive, and they quickly die. Why not buy your wife something that lasts, something "practical"? Then I discovered that wives *like* flowers; a corsage will stay in our refrigerator for a month, it seems!

Another example: Most men can live comfortably in a house not yet fixed up. But for a woman who's a homemaker, that's her area of expertise. The pastor wants his church to look well-run and nice; she wants the same for her home. His church is a reflection of him; her home is a reflection of her. So is her dress. If she wants things that make a house a home, or wants something to wear that makes her feel more feminine—and he squelches these as unimportant or unaffordable—she is left very frustrated.

Jackie stepped on the eyelash curler out of frustration and anger plus a heavy dose of "poor little me." It may have even been a manipulative move, without her being aware of it, to say, *Look how much I'm sacrificing for your church people.* Nothing was verbalized, of course, but there was a lot of anger.

The fact that they can laugh about these early-1960s days now says something, too: We must be careful as we get older not to lose touch with the struggles of younger couples in the ministry. Their difficulties may seem humorous or unimportant to us, but it is not so to them. The parent who watches his teenager fall in love is amused and says, "Oh, that will pass." It probably will—but it's very important at the time.

Things that look rather small to the Owenses now can be crucial to young couples who are insecure and struggling. These people need mentors who have lived through the stresses and are still sensitive to them. Mentor relationships don't last forever; in fact, Levinson's research shows they usually end after a while in hostility, anger, or distance. However, the mentor is still an invaluable person in the ministry as well as other careers.

When the Owenses were young, they also didn't have enough money. Too often we take young pastors, pay them inadequately, and put them in the most difficult situations: the church that's struggling or on the verge of collapse. That kind of place needs an experienced, capable individual with a strong backbone. If young pastors survive such an ordeal, then they get to go to bigger churches that pay better and function more smoothly! This all seems backwards.

A friend of mine told about going to his first church after four years of college and three of seminary. He had spent almost as much time in school as a physician.

His salary was set one evening at a public business meeting. Afterwards, during a coffee hour, the church chairman began exuding about his son who had just gotten a bachelor's degree and was now earning a handsome salary—far more than the figure just set for the pastor. "Isn't that exciting, pastor, that he landed such a good position?" My friend could only bear the irony in silence.

David Owens talks about consuming cartons of Rolaids. This is what happens to pastors who have no one to talk to about their stresses. My own pastor, who serves a church of thirteen hundred, has recently been through a similar experience. Two years ago, an arsonist set the sanctuary on fire. Throughout the long rebuilding program, there was a good spirit in the congregation; we didn't have a lot of dissension. But then a streak of unusual deaths came along. One young man committed suicide. A nineteen-year-old girl who had grown up in the church died of anorexia. (The pastor has daughters the same age.) The husband of the church secretary had a fatal heart attack on the way to church one morning. Several elderly "pillars of the church" also died.

One Sunday we all arrived to learn our pastor was in the hospital with a gastrointestinal problem. No wonder.

A parishioner who works there walked into his room and joked, "What are you doing lying there? You're supposed to be on your feet encouraging us!" I doubt the pastor found her comment very funny. Lay people often do not comprehend the pressures of the ministry.

The Owens story also shows the stress of fishbowl living. Even the location of their car is monitored! That's amazing—but I bet it isn't rare.

Here is a pastoral family trying to live up to others' expectations, and they're in a no-win situation. It doesn't matter what they do: If they go to someone's house for dinner, they're playing favorites; if they stay home, they're being cold and withdrawn. This sounds like what people said about John the Baptist and Jesus, doesn't it? One way, you're an ascetic; the other way, a "winebibber."

Jackie Owens apparently remained isolated until her husband got out of the pastorate for a while. Then she started wearing pearls again, went visiting people to sell Avon products, and got out from under the oppressive control. She didn't have to fit a role anymore, and as soon as that happened, it was like a load lifted.

It's very hard to blossom in an environment where you feel squelched and boxed in. If you were in the business community, you might buck it. But pastoral couples more often buckle under because, after all, "This is the Lord's work."

That makes it all the more important that we in the ministry help each other cope with the strictures, talk out our problems, diffuse our frustrations, and find effective ways to expand—not explode—the box.

FOUR

The Zimmers:
CLINGING TO A
DREAM

$\mathbf{I}$f you had been Ken Zimmer's high school guidance counselor back in Denver, you might have questioned his desire to train for the ministry. A middle-of-the-road student who got along well enough but stuck to the shadows, his leadership skills were not apparent. He was not a natural mixer with people, and he tended to hesitate before he spoke. When he finally opened his mouth, he usually had something thoughtful to say, if you didn't mind waiting.

Ken held to his course, however, went to Nazarene Bible College in Colorado Springs, and married Beth the week after graduation. It was a case of "opposites attract." Beth showed spunk, came from a highly educated family, wanted to succeed, liked to organize things. She was eager to get started in the ministry.

Their first opportunity, however, did not come for more than a year. They kept their secular jobs until a church in Pueblo invited them to a part-time position in music and young-adult ministry. It was a church of a hundred or so, with a pastor edging toward retirement. Says Ken:

We were to come and help him make something happen, revitalize the church. For a hundred dollars a month this young couple would sweep in and really light some fires.

Well, that wasn't quite what happened. That winter, in order to help the financial picture, the church asked me to organize a day-care operation. I got it going and found myself up to my waist in little kids twelve hours a day. Then the recession began to hit Pueblo, and enrollment dipped. The whole thing turned out to be a disappointment.

A string of supplementary jobs—selling water softeners was one—brought the Zimmers enough money to stay alive but a lot of frustration. By the end of the second year, Ken surrendered his title of assistant pastor and asked to be relieved of his weekday responsibilities in order to get full-time work. A baby had arrived by then, and the pressure to provide for his family overwhelmed his desire to continue in the ministry. He would continue teaching his class on Sundays and directing the choir on a volunteer basis.

Beth remembers her feelings:

> I was sure this would be temporary. I was young and naive and optimistic.
> But I felt bad for Ken, too. I'd never seen him so frustrated. The feelings of insecurity, you know—not making it at the church, your ministry not going anyplace . . . it was tough.

Letters to old friends in other pastorates produced encouragement but no offers. The only live option came from an unusual source: Ken's older sister, who had just been named pastor of a church in the small town of Frazee, Minnesota. "Come on up and help me," she wrote. "This church is just ready to blossom, and I really need your musical ability. It will be part-time to start, but with a lot of work, the position will grow. You can live with me in the parsonage to start. Expenses are quite low here."

Ken wasn't sure about that. For one thing, he dreaded patching together another combination of part-time jobs. Maybe they should just go back to Denver and get more education.

In the end, however, the pull of the ministry won. Pueblo

must have been just a false start. Frazee would put them on track.

The church turned out to be only thirty people on an average Sunday, and even Ken's sister was not drawing a full salary. The choir he had come to direct numbered six, not all of whom could read music. The Zimmers' compensation turned out to be free housing, and that was it.

Meanwhile, Beth was expecting again. For a month, Ken could not land a job. He finally found a carpenter who would take him on as a helper.

The "choir" soon proved unworkable, and Ken ceased rehearsals, to his sister's dismay. Communication between the two degenerated quickly.

I think she was really struggling for her own place in ministry as a woman. This was her first pastorate; she'd been in evangelistic work before and had had some disappointments, some real lack of respect.

But with every passing week, I was saying to myself, *This is the wrong place. We've blown it*. I tried a couple of times to tell her how I was feeling, but there just seemed to be no understanding.

Beth found herself the chief cook and maid for the household, and that caused its own tensions. She was not always sure whether her sister-in-law, who was used to the freedom of singleness, would show up for dinner. Yet Beth's ability to control the size of the grocery bill for the household was criticized more than once.

In Beth's reflections today, however, she tries to be generous:

I don't want to make her look like a mean person, because when I look back on it, I can see I was very young and immature, and way too sensitive. The pregnancy didn't help, either.

I've mellowed so much since then. I should have handled things differently. Now that we're in our own pastorate, I know what she was going through.

They still remember an incident that happened one Sunday morning not long after their little girl had been born. Ken was on the platform with his sister. But due to the low attendance, he also needed to fill in as an usher at offering time. Once the money was collected, he hurried to lock it away before returning to the sanctuary to lead a hymn before the sermon.

As he came through the side door, his sister was already at the pulpit, awkwardly filling the void with an offhand remark about "It's hard to find good help these days." Ken was both embarrassed and angry at the crack. It symbolized the whole disaster of their coming to Frazee.

But where should they go? Did *anyone* want them? Was his ministry ever going to get off the ground?

In May he called his mother in Denver.

> I hardly said anything; I just began to cry. I hadn't intended to do that, but . . . I just said, "Is there any way we could just move back to the house? I have no place to go, and we can't stay here. Talk it over with Dad."
>
> She said, "Fine—come on home." She could tell I was broken, emotionally exhausted.

Within a few days, they packed up and left. Ken's sister took their departure calmly. "Do whatever you think is best for yourself," she said. Before long, she too left the church, and the ministry.

The next year was again a season of retreat to secular employment: painting, factory work. Again Ken's feelers to the ministerial grapevine produced no invitations. The young family of four continued to live with his parents, who were gracious hosts, never pressuring them with hard questions. Inside, however:

> I said, "I've had it with the ministry. It's been six years, and we haven't gotten into it full time yet. I'm going to go to school and see if I can support myself [permanently] some other way."
>
> I felt no one cared about my being a pastor.

Ken looked at his wife and wondered occasionally if she wanted out of this marriage. After all, none of the dreams had come true. He was nothing but a failure. She had lots of steam, initiative; was she maybe thinking of leaving?

In fact, she was not. She was too busy with two preschoolers to entertain such thoughts. Her commitment as a Christian wife held firm. She says:

> The only emotion I felt at that time was relief that we were out of a demeaning situation. I didn't understand what had happened so far and figured we must be doing something wrong, but at least we had bread on the table.

Early the next year, an old college friend mentioned Ken's name to a pulpit committee in Sturgis, Mississippi, and he was called to come as a candidate. It was a rural church, but for the first time in Ken's experience, they talked of a full-time position. The Zimmers are there today.

There have been struggles in this church, and the growth potential is limited. But Ken has overcome his shaky beginnings.

> I said I was *not* going to quit here, go back to Denver, and be in the same spot again. I would stick it out. The Lord has taken all of that [early failure] and used it for our good.
>
> I remember the pastor in Pueblo telling me that pastoring is sort of like a child's punching toy. It gets socked and goes all the way down to the floor—but keeps coming back up again. In this work you have to have resilience.

Ken and Beth Zimmer's store of resilience lasted just long enough.

REFLECTIONS
by Gary Collins

Ken Zimmer is not a barn burner, but he is persistent. He's one of those people who doesn't show great natural talent but says, "I'm called anyhow." Mission boards encounter these people all the time. You can't knock persistence.

This couple's experience shows the pressure of parenthood on top of everything else. A lot of young couples don't recognize what adding a child does to a home. It's one of the most stressful things you can encounter. It was certainly that way in my own marriage. We like our kids and have good rapport with them. But kids are demanding; they take time and money; they squelch your freedom; they're messy; and you can't read books very well when they're around! If the pastor withdraws into his work when a baby arrives, the pastor's wife gets hit even harder.

The Zimmers decided to minister with Ken's older sister. I'm not completely comfortable with the idea of family members coming along to rescue relatives. Clashes often result, resurrecting a lot of baggage from the past. As a result, the relationship becomes difficult and the ministry suffers.

In this case, lifestyle conflicts developed. The sister's comment in church one Sunday ("It's hard to find good help these days") is an example of how casual remarks among family members can be very biting. This is passive aggression; she is angry, but instead of coming out and saying, "Ken, I don't feel you're doing your job," she says something pointed that also makes everyone laugh.

I remember hearing a student body president announce an all-seminary potluck one time. "Everyone be sure to bring a dish," he said. "My wife will probably bring her usual burnt sacrifice." Everyone laughed, including her (what else could she do?)—but what a powerful zap.

The more things fall apart in the Zimmer situation, the more Ken's self-worth is devastated. He begins comparing himself with his wife, who has more drive and steam, he says. Soon depression and discouragement appear. Because of a lack of communication, he fears his wife wants out of the marriage.

He doesn't actually know what she's thinking. He may have wanted to talk to Beth—but what if she said, "Well, you're right—

I *am* disappointed in you, and I've got too many creative things to do in life to stay around"? Rather than risk that, he doesn't bring up the subject. It's like going to a doctor to check on a mole. We think we'd rather not know the facts.

When my wife and I were expecting our first child, we went through a similar experience. I'd read books about women's sensitivity during pregnancy, and so I stopped sharing some of my pressures at work in order to make her life easier. Two years later, I found out what she really thought: *He's not talking anymore. He's not sharing about work. He doesn't find me interesting to talk to anymore. I'm putting on weight, losing my shape; he doesn't find me attractive anymore. I bet he doesn't love me anymore.*

That was all in her imagination; none of it was true. But as she said later, "I didn't dare bring it up for fear you would say, 'That's right.'"

Sometimes we let conclusions build in our minds that aren't valid. Consistent communication can keep this from happening.

FIVE

The Pacynskis:
NO WEAKNESS ALLOWED

The sickness that struck Greg and Kara Pacynski at the very beginning of their marriage was not enough to devastate in itself; a two-week hospital stay, and Kara's kidney infection was under control. But the baggage both husband and wife brought along turned the situation into a major blow.

They had met during Bible college days in Dallas, drawn to each other initially by their common interest in foreign missions. Greg was volunteering his time, however, with the youth group at a nearby church, and after graduation, a staff position was offered. He stayed on, waiting until Kara would finish school the next year.

The longer they dated, the more Kara learned about this handsome young man's past. His father, a former pastor in Idaho, had left church ministry when Greg's mother, a schizophrenic, finally had to be institutionalized. Greg was ten years old at the time, and there were two younger brothers and a three-year-old sister. Their father had since served as a missions board representative for the Mountain States. Greg says:

Basically, I was raised in a home without women. My mother never really functioned as a mother to us; I didn't have any role model of a wife.

I told Kara once that I didn't feel I knew how to love, because I'd never seen it in my parents' relationship. We almost broke up over that remark!

I wasn't a feeling-oriented person at all. Just the facts.

Greg's father, a man of principle and ambition, was most pleased that his oldest son was following his steps into the ministry. In some ways, he saw in Greg the replacement of his own work cut short. When Greg began edging toward the choice of a life's mate, his father was eager to size her up.

He found in Kara a goodhearted young woman who would do well in the parsonage, he thought. She did tend to wear her feelings on her sleeve, though, and to press her point a bit strongly at times. In a letter, he urged his son to check this carefully. "Make sure she's not the kind of woman who'll put your ministry on the shelf someday," he wrote, with obvious reference to his own disappointment.

Kara still remembers the day she and Greg were walking off-campus and he mentioned his father's letter. "He knew I was as dedicated to the ministry as he was," she says, "so it wasn't a big conversation or anything. But a fear was planted within me that day that I'd ever do something that would 'put Greg on the shelf,' ministerially speaking."

Just before engagement, Kara and her future father-in-law had an honest talk. She mentioned an earlier comment of his that had hurt her, and he assured her he had meant no ill. But later he wrote his son again to say, "If you're going to spend your life with somebody so sensitive, you may have a long row to hoe."

Says Greg:

My dad had a way with words!

I made the mistake of letting Kara read that letter, which only piled on more baggage. Every time she wanted to express her feelings on anything, she began to feel she was fighting my dad.

What he had written didn't bother me; in fact, I was *attracted* to her because of her warmth and expressiveness. I didn't particularly agree with Dad. But she thought I did.

The wedding went beautifully in Kara's home church in Colorado, and the happy couple drove off to a honeymoon week of skiing. By the next Thursday, Kara was not feeling well. She could not tell if the exhilaration of married life had overloaded her system or what. She felt tired and was running a low fever.

They left the mountains on Friday for the two-day drive back to Dallas. Her symptoms worsened. By Monday evening, her temperature stood at 104.6 degrees, sending Greg into near-panic. He knew very little, he felt, about a *healthy* woman, let alone one who lay still and burning, her lips cracked, and a low moan in her throat.

He ran to the apartment downstairs, where a nurse lived. She came up, began to bathe Kara's face and neck with cool washcloths, and after observing for an hour, said, "You really had better take her to a hospital."

A hospital? Greg had not even been in a hospital to have his tonsils out in junior high; he'd walked out of the doctor's office and gone home. One time playing basketball he had broken his nose, gone to have it set by a doctor, and returned to the gym the next day. The only hospital he had known was the state institution where they'd taken his mother. . . .

I remember sitting by Kara's bed the next day just shell-shocked. *Lord, is she going to make it? What's happening?*

I finally had to just release her to the Lord. I remember praying specifically, *I don't know what else to do, God. She's yours.*

The infection inside Kara's body was soon identified and brought under control with antibiotics. By the second Sunday, she was ready to be released.

Greg had to miss teaching his teen class in order to come get me. Here I was, being a hindrance to his ministry already in the first two weeks of married life. I was just overcome with guilt.

But talking about it would only make matters worse, I was sure. This was my problem, and I felt I just had to carry on, "sacrifice all" for the work, and try not to fulfill my father-in-law's prophecy.

Her mother came from Colorado to help Kara, who was weak and would need lots of rest in the coming weeks. Kara's plans to attend North Texas State and begin work on a master's degree had already been scotched. Greg, relieved to see her health coming back, turned quickly to the excitement of his youth group and was away from the apartment long hours at a time, including many evenings. He was also enrolled in graduate school.

After her mother went home, Kara remembers sitting one day all alone in a rocking chair ("the one piece of furniture we owned—everything else was donated by people in the church") and staring out at the traffic in the street below. "I had this overwhelming feeling that not one soul in the world had any clue how lonely I was. I couldn't do any of the things I had planned on doing. I was totally worthless."

Eventually she regained enough strength to begin working part-time in the church office. That provided a little money and also gave her fleeting glimpses of her husband. By January, she was healthy enough to begin school, which brightened her spirits considerably. Soon she was able to pick up the pace and begin matching Greg's stride by coaching a Bible quiz team, sponsoring the group's newspaper, and leading a girls' discipleship group.

The Pacynskis survived that first rugged year and gradually learned to share more openly with one another. The more Kara contributed to their joint ministry, the more she laid aside her early fears of derailing her husband's career. Greg became more expressive about his true feelings, and the influence of his father was placed in a larger context. The couple decided they would not feel compelled to agree with him at every turn but would strive to remain on friendly terms. That, in fact, is what has happened throughout almost twenty years of married life to date.

REFLECTIONS
by Gary Collins

The extended-family problem here is twofold: what the father expects, and what the daughter-in-law *thinks* he expects.

There is a lot of evidence these days to show that sickness is related to emotional tension. I'm sure Kara's recovery was lengthened by her worry about whether she was hindering Greg's ministry.

He, on the other hand, displays the typical seminarian attitude when he says, "I wasn't a feeling-oriented person at all. Just the facts." His father's judgment that Kara would do well in the parsonage is almost a commercial assessment: his son ought to acquire her as a good supplement to his ministry (she'd look nice around the house!). It reminds me of Nebuchadnezzar telling his servant to find Jewish lads who, as the Living Bible puts it, "have read widely in many fields, are well informed, alert and sensible, and have enough poise to look good around the palace" (Dan. 1:4).

All this sets the stage for problems.

Kara has been handed a script to follow, and she is hooked. Only later does she come to recognize she does *not* have to follow the lines others have written for her. She escapes major damage by regaining her health, proving her value in youth ministry, and most importantly, beginning to communicate about what is really going on.

When my wife and I were raising our children, our parents would come to visit occasionally. We have a fine relationship with them, but they would still make comments once in a while about "the way people raise their kids today." I got very up-tight about that, because the message I heard was *You're not doing it right.*

Then one day, I thought, *Wait a minute. I'm a big boy now. I've gone to school, gotten a job, I make my own money, I'm keeping my marriage together, we have children—I don't have to let my parents control me anymore. I'm on my own.*

Parents, church boards, and others can manipulate us, sometimes without even being aware of what they are doing. If we don't go along with their standards, we feel guilty.

My phone rang one day ten minutes before I was to teach a class, and a stranger's voice said, "Did you write a book called *How to Be a People Helper?*"

"Yes," I said.

"Well, I'm getting a divorce; tomorrow is the final action. What can I do to prevent it?"

I talked to the man for five minutes and, as you might expect, got nowhere trying to defuse a situation that had been building for years. So then he said, "I don't think you're a very good people helper. You can't even help me when I'm in a crisis," and he hung up!

For two days I walked around feeling incompetent. Finally a colleague said, "What's the matter with you?" I described what had happened. He replied, "That guy hooked you in an area of sensitivity and dragged you down."

Older pastors and their wives don't worry so much about the imposed expectations of others, but younger ones do. That's what happened to Linda Francisco in chapter 2; the minute the chairman's wife said, "Well, don't you have teacups?" Linda jumped up to follow the script. *This is important to this lady. I must produce what she wants. Oh, no—I'm not a very good pastor's wife.*

In the case of the Pacynskis, as soon as the health crisis was over, Greg quickly retreated to "the excitement of his youth group." He began to forget Kara and her needs.

Fortunately, she was able to get out and be useful on her own. His inattention was not as destructive as it could have been. God gives each of us gifts, not only in the church but in the home as well. We need to encourage one another, build one another up, and stimulate one another's gifts. Even pastors and their families can forget this.

As we look back over these several families in the early years of ministry, the major issues seem to be: self-worth, communication, expectations that come from self and others, idealism, insecurity, educational differences.

I do not want to say these years are terrible. There is a balance between unhealthy optimism and unhealthy pessimism. Too much warning immobilizes people. On the other hand, people can get swept up saying, "I can if I think I can!" and that's unrealistic.

The start-up years in the ministry have good and bad points. The Lord never promised it would be easy; we must take up a cross and follow him. But he doesn't put us in places where we will spend our whole lives being miserable, frustrated, and just surviving until transfer to another parish, retirement, or death. We walk between two extremes and must face the future with healthy realism because we trust in the sovereign, living Lord.

Part Two
CHURCH STRESSES

Hard Fact No. 1: The ministry never has been and never will be a nine-to-five job.

Hard Fact No. 2: Ministers who do not give attention to their marriages come to regret it.

Those two facts, of course, do not mesh very well. Both are true; both are acknowledged by husbands as well as wives. Neither fact is going to change. Pastoral couples simply have to accept them.

Most pastors find their own natural ambition heightened by what is at stake in the ministry: eternal destinies. One pastor tells an early experience that typifies the conundrum:

> *I was a youth pastor, and one day I had an impulse to stop and see a certain teenage girl. I didn't do it—and that night, she ran away.*
>
> *After that, whenever I'd get an impression to do something, I was afraid not to follow through on it. I don't think I did very well at taking a day off for seven or eight years.*
>
> *Finally, there were a couple of times at home in bed when Barbara said, "I don't know you" or "I don't feel a part of you. You're doing a great job as a pastor, but you don't know me."*

Dr. Dennis Guernsey, author and professor of psychology at Fuller Theological Seminary, says, "A pastor's wife is put in a terrible bind when the church becomes The Other Woman—but her husband isn't unrighteous for sleeping with her. No one considers this obsession immoral; he's 'doing God's work.' "

Most women bear this "affair" in silence for several years, until the pressure becomes intolerable. Then they confront. Richard Foth, who spent his first dozen ministry years pioneering a new church in Urbana, Illinois, tells about one day when he came home exhausted from a marathon of appointments. His normally placid wife (by then the mother of three young children) said, "Dick, I have a question. How come you give your life away to all these people you hardly know? They get the prime time—and we get the leftovers. Why do you do that?"

In the years following, he did some major reordering of his priorities. Now president of Bethany Bible College in Santa Cruz, California, he says, "The idea of ministry versus marriage is a false dichotomy. We must not pit one against the other.

"It's almost as if we've ripped Matthew 6:24 out of context and misapplied it to our work and our home—'No man can serve two masters: for either he will hate the one, and love the other; or else . . .' That's not what Jesus was talking about.

"Marriage gives rise to ministry. It is ministry's foundation. Out of our service to our wives we build a superstructure of ministry to the rest of the congregation."

The task for busy pastors, he concludes, is dual. "Building a marriage and a ministry is like trying to build a boat and a glider at the same time. They are both forms of transportation, they use similar materials—but they're different.

"And if you can't sculpt the prow of your boat to slice smoothly through the water—a substance you can see—how can you shape a wing to utilize the lift of the air, which you can't see? The shapes may differ, but the fundamental laws of physics apply to both."

The following case studies show couples working on both the glider and the boat. Some tell of difficulties at transition points—moving from one church to another—which is hard not only for Dad and Mom but children as well. Others deal with staff conflict; still others, with time pressures. All are examples of the way church stresses impinge upon home life.

"Reflections" in this part come from Louis McBurney, M.D., psychiatrist and counselor who operates Marble Retreat in the Colorado Rockies for clergy and their spouses who face crises.

SIX

The Ruches:
THE TOO-EASY
DECISION

"I don't think I ever had to make a really hard decision the first thirty years of my life," says Jim Ruch. He grew up the oldest of three sons in a staunch churchgoing family in Saint Joseph, Missouri, and his enrollment at one of the official church colleges on the West Coast was as much his father's choice as his.

Five years later (with a year out to travel on a denominational youth team), he graduated, married a blond classmate from Ventura named Sharon, and moved smoothly into seminary. His internship at a nearby church went well enough, and once he was ordained, the young family—three of them now, including little Kevin—moved to the Sierras to take a church at Sonora.

Says Jim:

It was an intimate community—you went to town and saw somebody you knew almost every block. The main show in town three months of the year was the high school football game. Everybody listened to the same radio station.

Plus, it was the summer home of several administrators and professors from the seminary, who'd come up to the mountains to relax. We had a great time together. I said I was going to stay there a long, long time.

That was right in line with the congregation's wishes; they liked this young couple and wanted to keep them longer than the usual three or four years. Sometime after Sharon gave birth to Mark, the church hit upon an incentive: a new parsonage. They invited the Ruches to help choose the floor plan, the carpeting, and the wallpaper. A spirit of pride began to grow in the church as the contractor began moving dirt and pouring the foundations.

The house was under roof, and in fact, the drywalling was already finished when an inquiry came from Wade Memorial in Kansas City. It was a church twice the size of the Sonora congregation.

Jim and Sharon had driven by the summer before while on vacation seeing Jim's parents, who lived only forty-five miles up the Missouri River. He'd even said to his wife, "Wouldn't it be something to serve here someday?"

Jim told the Kansas City chairman he'd call back within a week.

Twenty-four hours later, the wheels were already starting to turn. Kansas City . . . all the advantages of a metropolitan area . . . grandparents an hour away . . . a larger church, larger budget, larger facility . . . Jim dialed the chairman and announced he was willing to come out.

He mentioned the opportunity a few days later to a fellow pastor in Sonora. "Seems only natural," said his friend. "If God's calling you to something bigger, that's where you should go."

Candidating went well. The congregation's call to the Ruches was unanimous. A date was set for their coming to the Midwest.

The people in Sonora were of course disappointed when they got the bad news. It had happened to them before and would probably happen again. So they bore their feelings in silence. Jim had expected they would ask questions about where he was going and what it would be like, but no one seemed very interested.

The old parsonage had already been sold, so the Ruches spent their last month in town living in someone's mobile home. The church farewell was polite but restrained. Jim had promised himself he wouldn't get emotional, and he didn't. He said his good-byes, the moving van pulled away, and the family headed east.

One more smooth, almost automatic decision.

When they pulled onto the Kansas Turnpike at Topeka, excitement began to mount. A whole new challenge would soon be theirs. Jim checked his notes for the name of the trustee chairman who would meet them and show them to temporary housing. The church did not own a parsonage; the Ruches would be buying their own home in due time.

"Welcome to Kansas City!" said the man with a bit of a drawl as they stood together on the sidewalk outside the brick sanctuary. "How was your trip?"

It soon became apparent that he didn't have any housing arrangements made. He had meant to work on that but just hadn't gotten to it. They could do it together now, the three of them.

Jim and Sharon were a bit chagrined as they followed his car around the area, talking to three different apartment managers and asking about short-term leases. The Ruches finally decided to stay the next couple of nights with Jim's parents in Saint Joseph while the search continued.

By the weekend, they had landed an apartment and rented some furniture. Church ladies brought over a box of dishes and a box of pots and pans. "We felt like we were camping," Sharon remembers. "It was a little unsettling, since we'd always had a place to go to up till then."

The first Sunday morning went well, and that afternoon, Jim said to Sharon, "We'll probably do something with someone after the service tonight." She threw in an extra couple of toys to keep her preschoolers occupied at a restaurant or someone's home.

The crowd was small that night, and when the benediction was pronounced, the people seemed to move out quickly. There wasn't much standing around for chitchat. Soon it was just the Ruches and the custodian left. They said good-night and headed to their car a bit crestfallen.

Monday night Jim met with both the deacons and the Christian education committee and came away with a long "To Do" list. People seem relieved that the interim was now over; their new senior pastor would be grabbing hold, seizing many of the tasks they had had to tackle the past months.

On Thursday, there was a funeral to conduct. After the burial, people returned to the fellowship hall for a meal together.

> I remember a group at one table talking about having just heard J. Vernon McGee on the radio, and what a marvelous message he'd preached, and on and on. . . . I began realizing I wasn't the only voice in town! People had all kinds of different heroes.

There had been discussion in the pastor-parish committee, he knew, about his age. Some felt a thirty-year-old was too young for such a prominent pulpit. But the denomination had experienced a dearth of seminarians in the years prior to Jim's class, so pastors in the age group a bit older than he were at a premium. The church had finally concluded he was the best available.

That evening, Sharon was startled to find Jim sitting on the edge of the bed, head down, staring at the carpet. "Honey, what's wrong? Are you sick?"

He hardly shifted positions as he quietly said, "I can't do it. It's too much."

> I'd never seen him act like that in seven years of marriage. It was completely unknown to me. He just seemed overwhelmed with the task.
>
> We started talking—or at least *I* talked. I guess I got kind of

angry after a while. I mean, he'd brought me to this place he'd always wanted to go, and here I was sitting in this second-floor apartment with rented furniture and two little kids, and a husband who didn't think he could do the job we'd come to do!

She alternated between "Come on, you've got to at least give it a try" and a softer "You'll be all right; we know the Lord called us here, and I'll help you make it." The conversation ended with a decision to go see the district superintendent the next day.

The man expressed confidence in Jim's ability, told him he really didn't need to be afraid, and then asked a practical question: "Have you unpacked your books yet?" Jim hadn't.

"Well, I've noticed that sometimes when I get down," the superintendent said, "it's good to *do* something, work at a task."

Jim took his advice and spent Saturday arranging his library at the church. That evening his parents came down. They wound up kneeling together in a family circle and praying.

Jim preached acceptably the next morning and also carried through with an afternoon appearance before the membership committee; he and Sharon had to give their personal testimonies as part of becoming members of the church.

But the nights were another matter. He could not sleep. He slogged through Monday and Tuesday, accomplishing little. He didn't feel well. He was tired. He drove around the city supposedly looking at homes—but a couple of times just parked the car and sat crying. "I felt like I was in this big, big pit," he remembers.

By Wednesday, Sharon called her parents-in-law in Saint Joseph. "Something's got to be done. He is simply not functioning."

They drove down to attend the midweek Bible study and then announced afterward, "Jim, we're taking you up home to Methodist Hospital. You remember Dr. Clark; he'll know what to do to help you." Jim looked at them blankly and nodded.

Dr. Clark met them at the hospital late that evening, asked a few questions, and gave Jim some medication for sleep. The patient awoke the next morning feeling rested. Soon he was introduced to a psychiatrist named Stouffer, also a Christian, who listened to his account of the recent months and weeks. Jim says:

By the middle of that day, I was really feeling chipper. I began to have some ideas of things we could do at the church.

But that night, I came as close to suicide as I'd ever been. I felt like I was dying. I thought, *I've got these chemicals in my body, and I'm going to die by morning.* In fact, at one point I realized I had put my head in the toilet.

The psychiatrist came in Friday morning ready to send me home—and I told him all this stuff. He saw I was really in bad shape. He said, "We're going to have to take you someplace else."

Sharon arrived at the hospital that morning to see her husband—and was told he was being transferred to a private psychiatric hospital. She could not even drive him there; he would have to go by ambulance, strapped to a gurney, with her following along behind.

I was devastated. All the names being thrown around were unknown to me. I'd never suspected this kind of thing would ever happen.

What was I going to do? I basically had no home. All I had were my in-laws, who were very supportive. They knew where to go and how to keep this quiet.

But I'd never read books on depression or anything. I was feeling very alone.

One of her first tasks was to try to explain—from her limited knowledge—to the church chairman what had happened to their brand-new pastor. She didn't know where to start, so she gave up and arranged for the two of them to meet Dr. Stouffer. The district superintendent also sat in on the meeting. The doctor gave them his diagnosis and then said something very important: "He *will* get better. I want you to go ahead and do all the things you and Jim have talked about, even though he's not able to do them now. He *will* be able to function as a pastor again; this is not the end of the world." He closed by recommending some books for Sharon to read.

The chairman, fortunately, was an older gentleman who took the situation calmly. He arranged for a pulpit supply and assured Sharon of his support. On Sunday he simply told the congregation that Pastor Ruch was "ill and in a hospital up near his parents in Saint Joseph. He can't have visitors at the present time, but he'll be back with us soon." That was all.

Jim spent two weeks in the psychiatric hospital withdrawing from all pressure "and gaining about ten pounds," he remembers. Only the district superintendent and Sharon were allowed to see him.

> I had lots of time to think. Things like *I'll never be a pastor again. I'll surely never pastor HERE. . . . I'm thirty years old, and it's over.*
>
> God felt so far away. He wasn't there, or at least he certainly wasn't listening to me. I'd done something so awful he must have completely rejected me. I thought, *Well, I've got Sharon, and my parents—but they're probably thinking, "What in the world?"—this son they were so proud of.*

Next came the second-guessing of the decision to come to Kansas City. He must have been following his own desires, not listening to God back there in Sonora. If he hadn't come out here, none of this would have happened. If only there were some way to go back. . . .

That's it! Just tell the people here we made a mistake, and we're going back to California. That church hasn't called a permanent pastor yet—we can just slip back into that beautiful new parsonage, and everything will be fine again.

When Sharon arrived for her visit that day, Jim announced his new plan. She sat aghast listening to his instructions: pack up and get ready to head west, just as soon as he got out of the hospital. . . .

She and Dr. Stouffer managed to convince him that the past was over and done, and he'd have to stick with the present. The Kansas City church reinforced that message by paying his salary right on time. The chairman phoned one day to lend his encouragement and say, "Well, we're starting to make plans for Advent now. We're looking forward to having you preach on Christmas Eve." Tears came to Jim's eyes; they wanted him after all.

Rumors in the congregation were generally held in check. The most open incident came in a couples' group when someone said, "Let's pray for Pastor Ruch and his nervous breakdown."

A board member rose to his defense. "He didn't have a nervous breakdown."

"Oh, yes, he did," the first person insisted.

"No, he's just having a difficult time. But he'll be all right."

And that was the end of the discussion.

By the sixth Sunday after his arrival in town, Jim was back in the pulpit. The sermon was short that day, and the perspiration on the pastor's forehead was visible, but he managed to finish.

That evening, the phone rang.

"Pastor Ruch, this is Dr. Stouffer. How'd it go today?"

Pastor Ruch. The title so struck him that he couldn't answer the question for a few seconds. . . . So he really might be a minister again, here, in this very church.

In the following weekly appointments, Dr. Stouffer took him back to review the move from Sonora. Jim told how disappointed he had been at his former congregation's lack of interest in his ministry. He saw the folly of refusing to cry at the farewell.

For the next month and a half, there were good days and bad days. Bursts of initiative were broken by sags of despair. House hunting was a chore at times, and after they finally settled on a home, Jim didn't want to go through with the closing. "I can't commit myself to this," he told Sharon that morning.

His wife stayed calm but firm. "No, Jim, this is what we're going to do. Go ahead and get dressed; we must be down there at nine o'clock like we promised."

When she felt fearful, she tried to keep Jim from knowing about it.

I remember going for a walk one very foggy night. Jim had been real down again, and every time I saw him slouching and distant, I thought, *We're going to go through it all again.*

I walked and cried a long way. I didn't want Jim to know I was wondering whether we could put it together. At that point I was simply doing what other people encouraged me to do for him.

She had not lived in Kansas City long enough to have built any kind of personal support other than her in-laws, and even they were fairly new in her life. She needed someone to understand her, to reach out and say, "You must be hurting."

Such a person arrived on the scene at just that moment: a former boyfriend from California.

He was now an airline pilot. He called and invited Sharon out for coffee. He told about his floundering marriage, his money, and how he'd always remembered Sharon through the years. She recalls:

I was very vulnerable. I didn't know for sure if I had a husband who was ever going to be able to do anything. And here was Bob saying, "How nice it is to see you again; you're looking beautiful. . . ."

He began to call. And I was feeling a little flattered by it. It looked really good. I wasn't getting affirmation from Jim at that point; he wasn't seeing me as helping to pull him through his depression; I was more of a nag to him.

Eventually, Sharon realized she was facing a choice.

I had to say, "Look, Bob—I no longer want to hear from you. I do not want to see you, because I know I'm kind of weak just now." That confirmed my commitment to Jim, that through hell or high water we were going to make it. I was going to put my energy there.

Her statement did not keep the airline pilot from dialing her number again occasionally. But eventually, the contact ceased.

Meanwhile, Jim was learning more about what causes depression. He had never, as a pastor, dealt with anyone like himself. He found out a classic definition of depression is *repressed anger*.

> I'd never been an angry guy in my life, I didn't think. I didn't know what it was. Now I realized I had been genuinely angry at the people in California because of their cold shoulders and their lack of affirming my ministry there. I hadn't brought any kind of closure to the last pastorate. Nobody there had been blunt enough to say, "I'm really upset at what you're doing." And I had never said, "Well, it bothers me that you're upset."
>
> I hadn't brought that chapter to a close so I could be free here to start again. I wasn't recognizing that I was an emotional being; I just wanted life to go smoothly.

About that time, someone called from Sonora to say, "We heard you haven't been feeling too well. We just wanted you to know a candidate is coming to the church now, and things look very good. We're moving ahead here, and we sure hope things go well for you." That relieved a lot of pressure—and also told Jim he could forget about returning.

The last of the down days came in early December. He remembers a particular pastoral act—going to visit a recent widow—and suddenly "feeling like a pastor again." True to the church chairman's prediction, he *was* in the pulpit for the Christmas Eve service. By spring he was off all medication and had wound up his visits to Dr. Stouffer.

> It's been good since then to minister to other depressed people, to go into a psychiatric ward and say, "You're going to get better"—and know what I was talking about.

I'm sure I'll leave this church someday and go somewhere else. But when I do, I can tell you there'll be a lot of crying, a lot of feeling. Rather than dreading that expression, I now know it's part of being human. I think I have enough emotional health now to handle another transition.

Jim Ruch's ministry in Kansas City has turned out to be thirteen years running at this point, a stable and effective pastorate. His oldest son, a four-year-old when they came east, is now ready for college and will probably win a scholarship. Jim now serves on the denomination's pastoral guidance board, which oversees counseling services for ministers and hears disciplinary cases.

It is almost frightening to think how much worse his trauma might have been *if any one or more* of the following factors had been true:

- an unsteady wife
- a demanding or impatient church
- a too-busy district superintendent
- a domineering or martyrish set of parents
- an incompetent psychiatrist

This is a case where the supporting cast came through with honors. They said and did the right things at each turn, and as a result, Jim was quickly healed. Their prompt and sensitive action resulted in the salvaging of a ministry and perhaps a marriage.

REFLECTIONS
by Louis McBurney

Ministers are human beings, and the quicker they recognize their humanity, face their limitations, and get help when they need it, the sooner they begin to escape terrible consequences. Ministers are not perfect and don't have to be; they have legitimate needs for family, for support, for friendship. The church world must permit this, and ministers must accept it.

The Ruches are a normal couple who inherited the common assumption that bigger is automatically better. I am not saying they should not have gone to Kansas City; perhaps this was the right thing to do. But I have seen many other situations in which the Peter Principle has seemed to operate. A pastor has risen to maximum potential but hasn't been willing to stop there.

Why is it that whenever someone gets a call to a bigger church, it always seems to be God's will? At least that describes the cases I know about. Occasionally the call to a smaller church is said to be God's will, but not nearly as often.

I'm not sure I know all the answers to this, but I do know it's important for a person to know himself and what stage of life he's in. This fellow was around thirty years old—the time of establishing oneself as a more independent, productive person. The lure to Kansas City was definitely heightened by his own developmental needs.

He had a lot of things going for him in Sonora. The ministry situation there was far from bad. Yet something bigger came along that linked up with some private dreams. He had once said to his wife while in Kansas City, "Wouldn't it be something to serve here someday?"

Recently a man came here to the Retreat, a country boy who has now gotten into a big city church. The first thing he said in our group was "I grew up in the rural South and I'm really just a guy from the sticks." He's doing all right in his present church, but in his heart he knows he's out of place. He feels it every day and wishes he could go back.

It's the rare minister who can look at a larger opportunity and say, "But I'm comfortable; God can use me here," and be willing to stay.

This story also deals with separation. It was a lot easier for the Ruches just to drive away from their first church than to deal with their feelings. However, any kind of move is a loss. It creates a degree of grief, even if you're moving to a better situation or leaving tensions and problems behind. If you pack up the moving van without taking care of emotional closure, you're forgetting something very necessary.

And pastors move often—some say on an average as frequent as every two years. That can mean stacking up one grief reaction on top of another. Somewhere along the line, this catches up with pastors, as the loss snowballs.

When some of the things the Ruches had taken for granted didn't materialize in Kansas City—housing, for example, or warm fellowship right away—it contributed significantly to depression. There was anger about both ends: the cool send-off from Sonora, and the unsettled reception in Kansas City.

Jim didn't know how to deal with this. In fact, he didn't recognize his anger for quite a while. That's not unusual. The church world does not handle interpersonal conflict and anger very well. For one thing, our theology often says anger is sin, so any good spiritual person shouldn't have it. We are taught to deny it rather than deal with it.

So it gets expressed some other way. It sneaks out as bitterness, or criticism, or maybe depression, as happened to Jim Ruch. In one of M. Scott Peck's books, he says mental illness can be an attempt to escape legitimate suffering. Jim Ruch's mental crisis was born out of inattention to the processing of grief and anger.

Too many Christians have grown up thinking the New Testament demands we live in an ideal state—right now. Not someday, but in the present. There should be no conflict. No anger. No tension. If the church is as it should be, everything will be smooth.

That is just not going to happen.

The idea that a pastor should ever succumb to depression may strike some as unusual, but it is not. We see many such cases here at Marble. In fact, it is not unlikely that most pastors at one time or another are going to have to deal with some depression.

When that happens, one of the most needful things is to talk their feelings out. Jim Ruch was able to do this right away with a professional, but more than that, his wife appears to have been a very good listener. So was the church chairman and even the busy district superintendent. He told Jim to unpack his books. Physical activity is often important in dealing with depression, rather than sitting down and surrendering to the fatigue.

One aspect of depression is a sense of loss and of value, feeling unwanted, lonely, without purpose. Talking can help you identify what the losses are. It can also help you deal with the anger that is often (but not always) a part of depression.

Naturally, I encourage people not to be afraid to seek professional counsel for depression and not to be afraid of antidepressants. A lot of people say, "Well, if you go to a psychiatrist, he's going to fill you full of drugs." In some church circles, any kind of neuroactive drug is almost a sin.

Actually, the antidepressants are effective medicines that can often break the neurochemical effect of depression. They won't deal with the loss, anger, or relational issues, but they effectively treat the neurochemical and biological aspects. A short course of antidepressants can be very helpful. Illustration: Dr. Stouffer was able, by using drugs, to get Jim Ruch some sleep, which was obviously a prerequisite before other necessary things could happen.

Jim Ruch demonstrates his present healthy mind by being willing to tell the interviewer he once did something very irrational: he stuck his head in the toilet. He certainly isn't the only pastor who ever did something like that. We find in our group therapy sessions that such an admission is a healing factor. Other people say, "You did that too?" Or they say, "Well, last week I was so upset I sat with a gun in my lap thinking about blowing my brains out" or "The other day I lost track of where I was—I didn't know until two or three hours later where I'd been" or "I thought, *Boy, I'd just like to go get roaring drunk.* I've never been drunk in my life, but I sure thought about it. Why do I have those kind of thoughts?" The people all around the circle come to know that it's part of the human condition to do irrational things when under extreme stress.

Even being called of God does not exempt you. Look how many of the prophets in Scripture went off and did something kind of screwy. This is what I meant earlier when I said we do not have to be perfect all the time.

If you don't admit that, you may go the rest of your life thinking you're the only person in the whole universe who ever did such a ridiculous thing. Unless you're willing to risk being vulnerable and talk openly about yourself, the memory will grow and become a scar that may haunt you for a long time.

As a psychiatrist I've been in the unique position of hearing people's stories. I know now that virtually everybody did something once that has become his or her terrible secret. A tremendous relief comes from being able to unmask the secret and find out maybe it wasn't so bad after all.

SEVEN

The Wessingtons:
HANDLING THE "BIG BREAK"

Dwight Wessington was forty-one years old and happy in his pastorate at the Yakima Evangelical Free Church when he faced his major transition dilemma. At that point his career was well established: his seminary days had led to two years as an associate pastor in Boise, followed by fifteen in the top position at Yakima. During this time the church had grown from two hundred to more than twelve hundred.

A building program was under way; most of the funds had been raised. His stock in denominational circles had been steadily rising as well; he now chaired an important study commission on reorganization. A handsome, high-energy man with an electric smile, he kept his assortment of responsibilities humming with a minimum of strain.

Then came the day during a three-week vacation in the Canadian Rockies when Dwight called his office for a routine check. "There's a postcard here from Church of the Open Door in Seattle," said his secretary. "They want to know if you'd be interested in a telephone interview. Shall I just tell them no?"

Dwight had preached at that mammoth church a few years

back, when its pastor, Malcolm Sturbridge, was away. The sight of the cavernous sanctuary instantly leaped to his mind—the 120-voice choir, the 30-piece orchestra, the two services with nearly every one of the 2,000 seats filled both times, the sound control studio bristling with electronic gear to record the preaching for radio release over a nine-station network . . . *Church of the Open Door!* He had heard of Sturbridge's retirement announcement a month before, after twenty-two years there, but he'd never dreamed they might contact *him*. Of course, the list of prospects must be endless. . . .

"Well, let me see the card," he finally told his secretary. "Send it along."

When he told Barbara, his wife, about the inquiry, she was amused and flattered. She'd always known her husband was gifted; it felt good to have others even outside the denomination recognize that. But leave Yakima? How could they? She immediately began thinking of all the roadblocks.

That afternoon during a hike, Dwight bounced the idea off their two sons, fourteen-year-old Michael and eleven-year-old Joshua. The reaction was strong and clear: "Forget it. If you want to go to Seattle, put us in a boarding school or something. We don't want to go anywhere."

Barbara, an attractive woman whose skills as a hostess and diplomat have always been complimented, soothed them by saying, "Don't worry about it. That church is looking at dozens of ministers, and they'll probably never get down the alphabet to Wessington."

But they did.

Once the phone interview was over, Dwight and Barbara sat down to make a serious list of obstructions that would have to be cleared. Among them:

- The boys would have to come around.
- The Yakima building program could not be hurt.
- The denominational study commission could not be left in the lurch. Its work would have to be wrapped up.

Seven more entries filled the paper: ten doors in all that would have to open before they could ever make a move. Most of them were beyond the Wessingtons' ability to influence. The complications seemed invincible.

And besides, Church of the Open Door wanted its new senior pastor in place by *December,* less than four months away.

When they called and said they wanted me to come to Seattle for a talk, I went to my board to ask permission. They gave it. I also went to five or ten men I respected in the church and asked what they thought: "Am I free to talk to them? What do you think?" Some were brand-new to the church, including a new convert I had led to Christ. In some ways, I was probably looking for ties to stay. But it was also out of integrity, not wanting to betray anything I'd said or even implied. . . .

They all gave me permission, some after a week of praying about it.

The hardest question came from the wife of a young executive, who said, "Is this your climb up the corporate ladder?"

I didn't answer her until six months later, when I said, "A little bit . . . plus thinking it may be God's will, and a little bit of pure ambition to do what I can best do." It was a good question. I needed to hear it.

Sharing his opportunity created other problems for Dwight, however, as more people caught wind of what was happening. The congregation turned tentative, cautious. Some of the heavy donors to the building program felt betrayed. That made Dwight worry about whether he'd built this church solely on himself and his personality rather than Christ.

Each Sunday he looked out and thought about how much he loved these people. The vast majority of them had come to the church under his ministry. All those weddings and funerals, all that counseling . . . could he just walk away?

The months dragged on, and the Seattle committee seemed to go into a stall. Their December target date passed. Dwight was held in limbo. His staff in Yakima became nervous. The boss couldn't seem to make up his mind; where did that leave them?

> I lost credibility in their eyes because I didn't want to talk about it with them, and they didn't know that it was both me *and* the church [in Seattle] that was taking so long.
>
> For the first time in my life I experienced a major confusion. I lost sixteen pounds and really felt the weight of the decision, the guilt of leaving Yakima at this time, the horrors of trying to make a right choice. I read two or three books on the will of God. It was the first time in my life I'd been truly unhappy.

Friends in the denomination questioned Dwight's motives. Was he ditching his loyalty just to grab a star-studded pulpit?

Dwight knew the move would change his ministry drastically. The sheer size of the Seattle church meant becoming a preacher instead of an all-around pastor. In fact, maybe it would be even more like being a president, with all that staff to manage and all that budget to raise.

> Barbara was very supportive, very much the friend I needed to talk about it. We had always supported each other, but for the first time, she really held me together. That was different; I'd always been chairman of everything I'd been in.
>
> She just did a lot of listening, asking me questions, praying, showing me things she'd read now and then . . . but mostly just supporting me in love.

As spring moved on toward summer and the Seattle deliberations ground on, Dwight kept slipping into more and more confusion. He would soon have to declare himself on whether or not he was indeed willing to stand as a formal candidate. Barbara recalls:

> He would lie in bed in what I called his "coffin pose"—hands folded across his chest, just staring at the ceiling, anytime he had free time! He didn't sleep, and he didn't eat.

I had never seen him when he wasn't motivated. He'd always been so excited about life and what he was doing. Now it was a chore for him to move through a day. It scared me to see him just lie there looking at the light fixture.

Dwight Wessington, the man who had always prided himself on being a preacher of grace and liberty, was now paralyzed over the thought of missing God's will. He was also bedeviled by the possibility of hurting the church he had labored so hard to build. The son of divorced parents, he had vowed as a boy always to try to keep people happy, be the peacemaker, maintain a good atmosphere at all costs. The idea of causing pain to this dear congregation plunged him into agony.

Over the winter, his sons had mellowed a bit. Whether they had gotten intrigued with the idea of moving or whether they were just giving in was hard to tell. Barbara occasionally talked about how nice Yakima was, a medium-sized place where you didn't have to lock your doors. But she was not opposed to leaving if Dwight believed they should.

The bankers at first had said the church construction loan deals were off if a change of senior pastor should occur. But now they changed their minds. The study commission finished its report and presented its findings at the summer annual meeting.

Still, the risks were great. One of Dwight's ministerial friends looked at the long tenure of Malcolm Sturbridge and said, "Good luck—you'll be taking on a suicide mission for God. You are about to be the sacrificial lamb."

Finally, on August 17, with misgivings still rumbling inside his chest, Dwight stood on a Sunday morning in Yakima and said, "As many of you already know, my name has been in consideration by the pulpit committee of Church of the Open Door in Seattle. They have asked me to come as a candidate. Barbara and I will be spending the last eight days of September there, speaking two consecutive Sundays and meeting with a number of groups in the church the week in between. I ask your prayers."

He sensed the smell of a burning bridge behind him as he spoke, but he didn't know what else to do.

Some parishioners were listening with only one ear and came around to say good-bye. "No, I didn't say I was leaving," Dwight explained. "I just said I was going to candidate."

The fateful week arrived. He preached the first Sunday. Throughout the week, he must have spoken another ten times to various groups and fielded five hundred questions, it seemed. Over lunch one day with four committee members, he let slip an unfortunate remark. They had been talking about the balloting, which would occur on Sunday at the close of each morning service, and Dwight said, "Oh, I think I'll require a 98 percent vote, just to be sure." Everyone laughed.

Late Saturday afternoon, the phone rang at the hotel overlooking Puget Sound where the Wessingtons were staying. It was the vice-chairman of the trustee board. "The rumor is out that you're requiring a 98 percent vote before you'll accept. Is that true?"

"No, it's not true," Dwight replied. "Ninety-*four* percent."

Barbara looked up with a start. What was this?! Just that afternoon they had been marveling together at how each of the ten doors they had listed more than a year ago had opened. Even the boys were willing to move.

> That really made me angry. He wasn't being honest. It seemed like a test of God after everything else [had opened up].
>
> You don't know what it was like living with people [back in Yakima] who were angry at you because you'd even consider leaving—and having your husband so indecisive. . . . I'd had to absorb a lot of things during this time. I knew by now we probably couldn't turn around and say, "OK, you guys, we're staying."
>
> If he'd brought up a 94 percent requirement before, or even 96, that would have been fine. But after I had prepared myself emo-

tionally to leave . . . for him to add one more thing was just too much. I thought God would strike us dead right there!

They went to bed that night with the matter unresolved. The next morning, Dwight preached twice, and the ballots were collected. In the narthex afterward, the chairman told Dwight he'd stop by with the results around two-thirty.

Over a dinner of salmon in the hotel restaurant, Barbara again told her husband he was playing games with God. He had added an eleventh door at the last minute, and it wasn't fair. Dwight said nothing.

At two-thirty there was a knock at the door. The vote in favor of calling Dwight Wessington as senior pastor was 95.6 percent.

We drove back to Yakima that afternoon, and after a staff member preached in the evening service, I stood up to read my resignation.

It was a horrible, wonderful four weeks after that. I realized once again how close we had become to these people. The farewell Sunday came, and after an hour and a half of standing in line and crying and hugging, we drove to Seattle.

The cloud over my heart lifted during that drive. The next day I went into the office, and it was a new beginning. I've had pain since then, and hard decisions, and there's a great challenge here—but I've not had any remorse.

The pressure here is about seven times greater! And it's lonelier, since we haven't grown up with this church. But we know this is where we belong, and I'm grateful that God apparently didn't mind my tacking on one extra thing at the last. He must have known I needed it.

REFLECTIONS
by Louis McBurney

The Wessingtons' move from Yakima to Seattle came at age forty-one, which again is one of those transition periods in life. This too was a call to a larger place—a much larger place.

If I could discover what all goes into "finding God's will," I'd write a book about it and make a million bucks! Fred Smith said to me one time, "You know, maybe God's will is for you just to do what you enjoy doing."

When we came to start Marble Retreat, Melissa and I prayed, put out our "fleece," and so forth—and wound up with a very specific sense of call. But I think we might have come here just as comfortably if I'd said, "What would I like to do as a psychiatrist? Well, I'm interested in ministers. I'm interested in the church world. I've discovered ministers have problems. I think I'll just try to help them." We would probably have been just as blessed by God.

Maybe Christians ought to move toward a freer idea of call. Maybe our call is simply to become Christlike, and we can do that almost anywhere—here in the mountains, in a city, in a foreign country, wherever. I know people sometimes say, "I want to live up to my potential, and this bigger church will give me the opportunity to do that." Maybe it would be more honest just to say, "I'd really like that. I'd enjoy going there."

I've been reading in Acts recently, and it seems Paul went most places primarily because somebody was chasing him! He occasionally got visions and specific calls, but not often. Usually he was just running for his hide.

I realize I may be accused of heresy for questioning this, but I really do think we get into a lot of problems when we put the responsibility on God the way we do. If a move works out fine, then "it was God's will." If it doesn't work out fine, then it's not that we did anything wrong; we "must not have heard God's will right."

In this narrative, as the Seattle committee went into its stall, Dwight Wessington found himself experiencing a loss of power or control. He couldn't do anything to speed up the proceedings.

This often happens in the church, as we all know. It would be nice if you could always be in control, know what was going to happen, even control what was going to happen—but often that's not the case. You get stuck in situations where you are impotent.

This is one of the stresses ministers face: the feeling of powerlessness in church situations. When that happens, it is good to identify what is so important to you about wielding power. To many people, it's a need to feel a sense of worth; others want to be able to determine what's going to happen to their destiny. All this touches one of our basic developmental stages: dependency versus autonomy. We first struggled with that as two-year-olds, trying to be independent and in control of ourselves while also having to admit dependency. Well, at forty-two, we *still* have realistic dependence. No wonder we feel tension when in a limbo state.

The more we can realize we are *never* in total control and begin to place our faith more squarely on God, knowing he is there and hasn't abandoned us even if things don't work out as we want, the better we can cope.

Another aspect for men particularly is that a lot of our male identity has to do with power and the ability to effect change. When we lose power and control, it threatens our maleness. But in fact, we are not less valuable in God's eyes. I am not less of a man for being vulnerable.

Resigning a pastorate was tougher for Dwight Wessington, as the story explains, because of his need to please everyone. He had grown up in a home where there had been divorce, and so one of his early marks of value as a person was to be a peacemaker and please everyone. Now, as he looked at his options, he knew some people would be displeased if he went to Seattle.

If you hold such a factor to be important in your personality, church stress will be magnified a hundredfold. You run into situations daily where you're not going to please everybody. You can work yourself to death if you don't deal with that.

The actual separation in this story, once Dwight made up his mind, was handled beautifully—a refreshing contrast to the Ruch story. Dwight talked about what was going to happen at every stage along the way. They had a farewell dinner where people were able to cry, hug, and find closure. Too often this doesn't happen for churches and pastors.

At the very end he mentions the pressure and loneliness he faces in Seattle. This is often the case after a pastor moves; he feels dislodged and not belonging. It takes awhile to build up close relationships—probably three years or more under good circumstances.

And yet, many ministers move again before they ever have a chance to do that. I've heard some ministry couples say they never felt this was *their* church. It belonged to the people. Some parishioners would even comment, "You're going to be leaving eventually; we've got to stay. This is our church. You're only here for a little while." The pastor and spouse felt like transients, migrant workers. This created stress, and it occurred because the ministers didn't take the time—or get the time—to settle in and belong.

The Wessingtons, of course, had been in Yakima fifteen years; this was most certainly "their church." That is part of what made leaving so hard. But I feel confident they will build solid relationships in Seattle, assuming they stay long enough to nurture them.

EIGHT

Craig McKnight:
HELLBENT FOR
HOCKEY

The trauma of transition is some-times a major mortar attack on pastoral offspring. Husbands and wives may be agreed that a move is within the plan of God for their lives and ministry, but convincing the kids can be tough. That can make the grownups start questioning their earlier decision.

Jerry and Arlene McKnight thought they had handled the thousand-mile move from Winnipeg to Dearborn, Michigan, as well as could be expected. No one likes to uproot, of course, and crossing the border to begin ministering in the United States was an extra consideration. But the opportunity as associate pastor of this large Lutheran church was exactly what Jerry was cut out to do.

Both husband and wife had known rocky adolescences; they had not even become Christians until after their first child, Melissa, had been born. That had made them eager to raise their children with care. They also wanted to implant a positive attitude toward Christian service.

They could understand the reluctance of Craig, their sec-ond child, to leave Canada in the middle of high school. His younger brother, Kurt, was not as upset—but Craig had a hockey career on the line. A muscular blond left wing, he had scored forty-two goals and made thirty assists as a sopho-more. Did American high schools even know what hockey was?

All during that fall, as the Michigan church concluded its search and extended its call, the debate at the McKnight house churned. Craig resisted strongly. But one day as Jerry was in the car with him, he said, "I've been thinking some more about it, Dad, and if you really think it's God's will for us to move, I'm willing to do it."

Jerry was grateful for that and said so. As things turned out, Craig's junior season was salvaged after all. The house did not sell for several months. Arlene and the children remained behind in Winnipeg, while Jerry began his work in Dearborn, flying home a couple of days every two weeks. This went on throughout the winter.

Jerry found out the local high school *did* have a hockey team, although as winter sports go, it was no match for basketball.

The family finally moved south at Easter break. Jerry remembers:

> By this time, Craig had played another stellar season—and the old resistance was back. His coaches were talking about next year, his senior year: it was going to be his greatest. The drive down from Manitoba was very quiet, I recall.

Three weeks later, on April 17, Craig turned eighteen—and issued a shocking announcement: He was going back to Win-nipeg. He'd been in touch with the coaches, and they were sending him a ticket.

The family was not even fully unpacked yet, the blur of names and faces in a new church responsibility was still swirl-ing—and now this. It was a Friday night. Arlene began to cry, while Jerry paced the floor weighing his options.

> What was I supposed to do—stand in the doorway and wrestle this big 190-pound kid to the floor?

I asked him where he was going to live. He gave a name. The family was absolutely pagan.

He'd also been involved up there with a certain girl we were less than pleased with.

But his mind was made up.

Jerry finally decided he was powerless to stop Craig from going, and he didn't want him leaving alienated. He agreed to drive his son to Detroit's Metro Airport. Craig awkwardly told his mother good-bye, brushing aside her tears and saying with mock maturity, "Get ahold of yourself, Mom!" Father and son then headed off into the night.

"That was about the saddest moment of my life," says Arlene softly, a mother who never aspired to be a pastor's wife in the first place, let alone leave her country or face the ramifications of a headstrong son.

Near the airport, Craig had a question. "Is flying safe?" He'd never been in an airplane before.

"Yeah, it's safe," Jerry replied. "But I still can't believe these people sent you a ticket. I'm going to pull up to the curb and wait; you go inside, and if they actually have a ticket waiting for you, wave it to me."

The boy piled out of the car, grabbed his two suitcases, and went indoors. Five minutes later he was back . . . ticket in hand. "Here it is," he said, looking straight at his father. "I love you." And he was gone. Says Jerry:

> It was raining. I cried all the way home. I was mad. Mad at God for moving us to Michigan, for letting this happen, all kinds of things.

In a smaller church, such a departure might have set tongues to wagging and raised some uncomfortable questions for Jerry and Arlene. In this large metropolitan congregation, however, it created no ripples. The McKnights were left only with their personal feelings of regret and worry.

Craig had left the control of his parents, but he had not moved beyond the range of God. Sometime in early July, he had a spiritual experience that reordered his values. He broke up with his girlfriend. He decided he belonged back with his family. "I'm coming back home," he said on the phone.

"Great!" Jerry replied. "We're coming up next month to pick up the rest of the furniture we left in storage, so you can help me load and then ride back with us."

But by the time they arrived, the hockey coaches had been at work again. Plans for the new season were now in full bloom. A new living arrangement had been worked out. Craig was wavering.

The night before they were to head south, he said, "Well, I've changed my mind; I'm going to stay." That was more than Arlene could swallow.

> I guess I really flipped out. I zinged a pillow across the room and screamed, "I'm so mad at you!" He jumped up and ran out the front door. Kurt ran after him—in his underwear! It was a wild scene.
>
> I guess I go too much on my emotions. Jerry is more steady than I am.
>
> But we had to leave him there again.

In October, Craig was finally felled by that most basic of human needs, especially in a growing kid: his stomach. He was an avid body builder, able to bench-press four hundred pounds, and his hosts simply couldn't—or wouldn't—replace the calories as fast as Craig burned them up.

Suddenly the memories of Arlene's kitchen took on a new warmth.

"This is ridiculous—I'm not eating!" he complained on the phone. "They don't feed me. I'm coming home."

Jerry burst out laughing.

"Are you sure?"

"Yeah."

"Home to stay?"

"Yeah. I'll play for Dearborn High this season."

By two o'clock the next afternoon, a ticket had been sent, and Jerry and Arlene stood waiting at a Northwest Orient gate for their son. Out came a disheveled young man in jeans only a mother could love. Arlene reached up to plant a kiss on his cheek anyway, and he did not resist.

Unfortunately, the phone calls to Winnipeg did not cease, and once again Craig began talking about returning. That was enough to spur his father into direct protest. He called the high school principal. "Tell your guys to knock it off," he demanded. "The kid's gone through enough. They're worried about a hockey season; I'm worried about his life." That put a stop to the wooing.

Craig's senior year on the ice did not go particularly well, the style of play being different in several ways than he was used to. Jerry caught the blame for that, of course.

But in the end, Craig managed to graduate and went on to do well in college. He is close to his parents still, as an adult, and has maintained his Christian walk. The rupture of his teen years may have scared everyone, including him, but it proved to be temporary.

REFLECTIONS
by Louis McBurney

It's important to recognize that family situations, health reasons, and many other things are important to consider in evaluating a call. Certainly a son's hockey career is not life-and-death, but it's still important. All we have to do is look back at our own adolescences to realize how very important those kinds of things can be to a young person. I have counseled any number of people who felt their whole life had been scarred and traumatized by a move during adolescence, whether because of the ministry or some other reason.

PKs aren't the only kids who have to uproot, of course. A lot of people in our culture do it. But that doesn't make it ideal, even when the transition is smooth. Military kids often seem to handle their transitions very well, but you talk to them later in life, and they say things like "I never had a really close friend. I always knew I was going to be leaving, and it was too painful to go through the separation."

Pastors must not forget they *do* have a choice about whether to accept a call. Too often I see men and women develop almost a compulsion: "Here's a call! What do we do? We *can't* say, 'Well, no, we don't feel this is the time for us to move.' " On the inside, they are thinking, *We'll never get a chance like this again.*

That is a fallacy. If a couple is doing good ministry, chances are they'll be called for many years. Even if they keep saying no, chances are offers will keep coming if they're ministering effectively. They need not be impatient.

Pastoral couples in the shoes of the McKnights need to remember that it is all right to share these hurts with a congregation. There may not be an immediate response of warmth and care, but that is all right. People are sometimes uncomfortable with pain and distress and will seem to back away. To the hurting person, that feels like rejection and disinterest. It's not; it's usually fear. The people don't know what to do or how to handle things.

At that point, it's important for the hurting person to go another step and say, "I need to talk to you; please wait and listen." Take more initiative; don't just sit and say, "Boy, I wish somebody cared." The carers are there; they're just afraid.

NINE

The Franciscos:
AN ERROR
IN JUDGMENT

When after four years Jeff Francisco began to think about leaving Hooper, Nebraska, he knew any transition would have its perils. Linda was getting along well now, her middle-of-the-night emotional crash not much more than a memory (see chapter 2). She had stabilized to the point of feeling comfortable in this little town. If she had to get used to a new setting, would terror strike all over again?

A young couple in the church said to Jeff one day, "You know, you've taught us so much about being open and caring for one another. But if the time should ever come that you leave our church, we'll probably leave too."

Jeff and Linda talked a lot about that remark. It symbolized their hunch that this congregation, given its rural traditionalism, would probably never move fully into the deep ministry to one another that was so central to their idea of Christianity. People were attracted to the two of them personally, but the *concept* wasn't sticking. Would another ten years make it stick? Probably not.

Jeff put his name in the denominational hopper, and soon inquiries began to come. He finally candidated at a church in Branford, Connecticut, that already had small groups going.

This would mean returning to beloved New England, and although Branford was a small town on Long Island Sound, it was less than a dozen miles from all the culture of New Haven.

The church had a parsonage but did not insist the Franciscos use it. If they wanted a housing allowance to buy their own home, the parsonage could be sold. Any arrangement was fine with the board.

Jeff and Linda, while on their candidating visit, drove by the parsonage one gray, rainy afternoon. A car was in the driveway (a member was doing repairs) so they stopped for an impromptu tour of their own. Linda was not impressed. The empty rooms seemed dull in the chilly air, and there were no lamps in the bedrooms to give a true picture. "There's no warmth to this house," she said to her husband. "Let's get something different."

That settled the matter.

They spent some time with a realtor and picked out two houses they liked. If a call were issued by the church, they would place a bid on one or the other.

The call did come through in a week or two. Jeff accepted and began planning a return trip to Connecticut to arrange housing. Since the church had a parsonage available, it was hardly obligated for this second airfare, and the Franciscos, after checking their bank account, decided Jeff should go alone.

Today, they give an urgent word of advice to other couples: "*Never* send one spouse to pick out a home! It can be extremely hard on the marriage."

Jeff arrived to face a shock: Both houses spotted earlier were now sold. The second one, in fact, had gone only the night before he arrived—after sitting on the market for ten months. Suddenly he was back to Square One.

I knew I had to pull this off right. In light of what Linda had been through the last move, I really needed to make her happy.

She was *not* interested in the parsonage; I knew that. We had also talked about the fact that with the kids growing up now, we didn't want a fixer-upper. We didn't want to sink a lot of time into remodeling, as we had done in Hooper. The house had to be livable right now.

The trouble was, homes here were smaller than in Nebraska— for half again as much money.

Their house in Hooper had a tentative buyer, pending the sale of his other home. So armed with an equity figure, Jeff went to work again, shopping. He ended up this time with a realtor who was a strong talker, an aggressive type. She showed him a number of homes, including one on her own lane that was "just perfect for your family, and a great opportunity." The yard seemed small, but then again. . . .

Jeff wasn't sure. The price scared him. He called Linda at one point and said, "Maybe I should go over and see the parsonage again." She quickly squelched that idea.

So he made an offer on the newer home, and it was accepted.

On the plane headed west, he was seized with a case of cold feet. *What have I done? It really is too expensive. And it only has three bedrooms, and we have three kids.* Upon landing in Omaha, Jeff shared his misgivings with Linda.

The next morning he called the realtor to back out. "You can't do that!" she shrieked. "You'll lose your earnest money, and they could take you to court." That was not true, legally, but the Franciscos didn't know better, and they certainly did not want to launch their ministry in Branford with a lawsuit. Jeff said they would stick with the deal.

Moving day arrived about the same time as the Hong Kong flu, which was sweeping the country that year. By the time the plane landed in New York on a Tuesday, Linda was almost delirious with fever. She was helped to bed and nursed through the next five days, barely making it up for her debut as the new pastor's wife on Sunday. The next day she accompanied Jeff to the local bank to sign for a bridge loan of twenty thousand dollars, since the Nebraska house had not yet sold and they had no other down payment.

Linda remembers seeing her new house for the first time:

> I thought, *Wow! For us??* All of a sudden I realized Jeff, in his eagerness to make me happy, had overcompensated. I hadn't wanted him to be burdened with an old junker, but we probably didn't need a five-year-old house either.
>
> I didn't dare tell him this, though. He was already hurting, and anything I would say would simply put salt in the wound.
>
> That caused kind of a silent rift to grow between us.

The family moved into the church parsonage temporarily, until closing day—and found it far more engaging than it had looked that gray, rainy afternoon. It was old but well cared for, and the whole kitchen had just been redone. Linda realized she could have been happy here after all.

But it was too late. Jeff and the church board were already opening the bidding process for the parsonage, and several well-connected young couples in the congregation had their eyes on it. Jeff finally had the pain of presiding over the selection of an offer twenty thousand dollars less than he and Linda were paying—for less of a house.

Meanwhile, the deal back in Nebraska kept stalling. The buyer's home did not sell, and his contract to buy meant nothing until it did. Jeff regretted not having put a similar contingency clause in the contract *he* signed. "I thought I was showing my faith: 'God always works things out; he's in charge of moves.' Maybe it was just naiveté."

Jeff wanted to share his dilemma with older, wiser leaders in the church but feared it would make him look bad. After all, hadn't they given him the option of living in the parsonage? He'd made his own bed.

Four months down the line, the church did offer to replace the bridge loan at the bank. They set a lower rate of interest and agreed to a flexible repayment schedule. Nevertheless, the Franciscos still found themselves surrounded by creditors: the Connecticut bank that held the basic mortgage, the church that held the second mortgage, the Nebraska bank with their old mortgage as long as the house there went unsold, plus the federal government, which had granted them two college loans.

The house in the small Nebraska town, although rented intermittently, did not sell for *more than four years*. In the meantime, savings dwindled away. The church loan principal of $20,000 went unreduced and in fact was swelled by an additional $8,000 of deferred interest. Last year Jeff finally requested no salary increase, the money going directly toward the loan instead.

> It has been a financial mistake I've struggled with ever since. It started me on a downhill spiral of emotions and hurts and regrets that has gone on and on . . . until the events of the past year finally brought me out of it.
>
> I couldn't be honest, put my cards on the table, and tell the church, "I am really in a mess. Help me out." As the shepherd of the church, I just couldn't.
>
> The anguish has been to be caught in the middle and not to see any long-term solution. Not that we've had to come down to eating beans and franks every night—it's rather a deferred loss. Instead of building financial security, we're steadily going the other direction. How is it all going to work out? I don't know. All I can see down the road is a great loss, and we just have to absorb it.

Real estate values in Branford, as in much of the nation, peaked out about the time the Franciscos bought, and have stayed relatively flat since. So to sell their home would generate very little equity, especially in light of the high dollar Jeff paid for the house in the first place. The options are few—which is what has frustrated him from the beginning. Given Linda's wishes, he felt his hands were tied, and once he made a disastrous choice, there has been no way to repair the damage.

What have been the spillovers of all this? How have the financial reverses befouled the marriage and the public ministry in Branford?

Jeff and Linda give a number of candid answers. They speak without bitterness now, but with realism. Linda begins:

This whole thing turned out to be destructive to our relationship for more than three years. I knew there was no way in the world I could please Jeff. Nothing I said lessened the hurt, the anger, or changed the picture for him.

Night after night he would lie awake and agonize—even cry quietly—wondering, *What have I done? How are we ever going to recover? How could I have made such immense errors in judgment? God, where were you in all of this?* It took a tremendous toll.

He became aloof, judgmental, driven. He clenched his jaw and went from one day to the next.

When a decision needed to be made, sometimes he would vacillate between "Let's make this together" and *"I'm* going to decide." If we tried to work it out together, it seemed more like placating; we just role-played. The spontaneity and trust and deep-founded communion weren't there.

Jeff, the affable former youth worker whom even a busload of rowdy teenagers could not ruffle, now carried a smoldering anger. He was not the type to yell and argue with Linda or anyone else, but inside, he berated both himself and his wife. In the church, he found it hard to smile at the people who had reaped a windfall when the parsonage was sold. They had done nothing wrong, of course, but Jeff could not seem to remember that. He avoided asking them to help with Sunday school or organize a work day. He'd rather tackle the job himself.

The more I realized everything was in cement, and our finances were only going to get worse, the more depressed I became. I was missing the spark, the joy of the Lord—but still trying to be a minister. A lot of the fun and spontaneity had been zapped out of me.

I tried to find those who would be sympathetic, but what could they do? I went to the bishop and tried to share where I was, but I wasn't direct enough to say, "Is there some way you can help the church understand we are sinking in debt? We're just losing money hand over fist. Is there any way they might see it as a ministry to us to postpone the interest, for example?"

Who knows? The Lord makes beauty of ashes, and I hope he will. I hope I can learn to praise him more and thank him for what he teaches us through times of depression, as Isaiah 61 says.

Linda's role as a full-time mother had to be sacrificed. She dusted off her credential and signed up to substitute-teach in the local high school. It was one small way she could help rectify the problem she felt half-responsible for causing.

It was worse than awful. The stories I could tell of what kids do to substitutes in high school these days would turn you gray. This particular school didn't support subs very much. I hated every moment of it. I hated worse the *anticipation* of having to go . . . because it was the penance I had to pay.

And I couldn't refuse to go . . . because I couldn't let Jeff down any more. I would just totally knot up when that phone rang in the morning. I thought, *No person should have to endure this. This is no way to live.*

Linda breaks into tears as she describes this year and a half. She was driven to the classroom as much by her own guilt feelings as by Jeff's insistence, but all the same, it nearly destroyed her.

Finally she landed a teacher's aide position in the grade school her oldest daughter attended. It was ludicrous in a sense—a person with a master's degree working for minimum wage. But at least it was a reprieve from the halls of Branford High.

With such turmoil in her days, she could hardly manage to paste on a pastor's-wife smile for evening entertainment of church members. Jeff had grown up in a wide-open home that freely welcomed visitors.

Hospitality isn't my primary gift, and under the circumstances, there was just no way I could be another Mom Francisco like he remembered. But I felt that whenever I said I couldn't manage dinner for someone that weekend, I was really letting him down.

I didn't have the energy to keep up with him. And I think if anything, he was being *driven* by his hurts. He seemed to be thinking, *Well, maybe I'm a financial failure, but I'm going to be a success otherwise in the ministry if it kills me.*

The aloneness of both husband and wife was occasionally broken by talks about their predicament. Jeff would wonder aloud whether Linda cared all that much about their debts; her words about trusting the Lord seemed glib to him. She professed a belief that God would somehow help them weather this storm, but he had trouble hearing that.

The Lord had to deal a lot with my pride. After all, there are businessmen in the congregation who have had financial pressure, too, good years and bad, and the high interest rates hit them, too. So we were just one of the club, I guess.

Outside support and friendship came Linda's way through a women's group at the church. Eventually, Jeff met a parachurch worker in town with whom he could be honest. This relationship grew into a vital, healing bond.

Still, at times Jeff talked of leaving Branford. How that would solve anything he didn't know, but at least he would be rid of the physical reminders of his mistake. Linda recalls:

The first couple of times he said that, I nearly panicked. I said, "Jeff, whatever is happening or not happening between you and me—it wouldn't be different anywhere else. If we don't resolve it here, another location won't help. And probably we'd go to the cleaners again if we move right now. It's never cheap to move!"

And he'd grudgingly say, "Awright."

I would just pray, *Lord, give him and give us the encouragement to carry on.*

Once in a while, he'd even mumble about leaving the ministry. I'd bait him about that . . . but then I'd get scared, thinking, *If I'm not a pastor's wife, who am I?*

Two events helped Jeff Francisco stop living in his remorse and look toward the sky again.

The first was the sale of the Hooper, Nebraska, house. After four years, a buyer was finally found. The bottom line amounted to a $15,000 loss on their investment, but at least they were able to close that chapter of their lives.

The second was a spectacular car accident in which Linda and young Nathan were almost killed. Driving along a shoreline ridge one day, she lost control of the car and plunged forty feet down a steep slope. She barely managed to get herself and her son out before the car burst into flames.

Nathan had only bruises and cuts, but Linda sustained massive internal injuries plus a concussion. By the time she was wheeled into surgery, she had lost consciousness and her blood pressure was dangerously low. She was on the operating table four hours.

Suddenly, like a cold front sweeping the haze in front of it, turning the air crisp and clear, the accident changed everything. For the next five days Jeff had no time to think about the murky past; he was on his knees pleading with God for Linda to pull through. Though her life had been spared, the question of permanent brain damage lingered. The congregation rallied to provide child care and meals while Jeff sat hour upon hour at the New Haven hospital.

> I couldn't help thinking what it would have been like to have lost her. The message was so strong in my mind: "Love one another. Be thankful for one another. Be thankful for your kids, your wife."
>
> The Lord allowed the accident, I believe, to shift my focus, to help me see his graciousness and goodness and mercy, and his power—the fact that he's in control.

Linda came home from the hospital nine days later and spent a month recuperating. In the end, she sustained no ongoing disability. When people came to visit and said, "You must be wondering why such a thing had to happen to you," she said the question had not even crossed her mind.

I *knew* why. It wasn't a vindictive thing, a punishment, or anything other than an opportunity for the Lord to teach me to trust him and praise him. He wanted me to learn more about those areas. I needed to grow there.

And Jeff and I needed to grow there together. We hadn't been doing much praising together!

I don't know that I would wish away these hard times. They've brought growth to us in ways that never would have happened otherwise. We can understand people in pain or in depression better than any clinical training would have taught us.

The ultimate irony came the day Linda went out to the mailbox and found a thirty-five-dollar traffic ticket—for crossing the center line! She came inside laughing to show her husband.

Then a sobering thought struck her. "I wonder what it would have done to you if you'd received this ticket today, and I hadn't been here to laugh with you," she said.

Jeff put his arm around her as he replied, "To have my wife, I'm *glad* to pay thirty-five dollars."

When it comes to paying their larger debts, they have stopped worrying about them. The accident has taught them that God still knows where they are, is concerned for their good, and will not let the pressure get out of hand. The lessons of the past five years have been both practical and spiritual, creating a stronger union between them as one result.

REFLECTIONS
by Louis McBurney

Jeff Francisco's financial problems are not unusual; a significant number of ministers who come here to Marble Retreat are in similar straits. They "trust the Lord to provide" (and he does), but often they have made the Lord's job considerably more difficult by failing to seek professional advice!

If Jeff had asked an attorney or a businessman, or another realtor, he might have saved himself lots of grief. Ministers seem to have the notion that because they're professionals with all this responsibility as a pastor, they dare not confess they don't know something. That can lead to disaster.

As the situation worsened for the Franciscos, they found it almost impossible to deal with their anger at themselves, at each other, at the church about the sale of the parsonage, at the real estate agent, at the economy, at God—they never really dealt with these. That is why serious depression set in.

Jeff worked all the harder to succeed at *something*. That may have been a good way to handle his feelings, to some degree. But the couple could have had a healthier relationship by dealing constructively with their feelings of tension and guilt through the help of a counselor, a friend, or someone else. This is another illustration of what not to do when you meet up with significant negative feelings. Don't just try to deny them.

Linda's ordeal of substitute teaching was again worsened by not dealing with the feelings. She didn't feel she could talk about her anger because of the guilt involved. It seems to have paralyzed her from seeking any other alternative.

How do you break this kind of spell? You reveal the feelings. Once that happens, you are free to look at options and talk about other courses of action. It's amazing how talking about what's going on diffuses the impact. If Linda had talked about her feelings with her husband or someone else, substitute teaching may still have been unpleasant, but the intensity of the feelings would have been released.

However, it is true that people in stress are often immobilized, unable to see options, or move in a more healthy direction.

TEN

The Pacynskis:
FIRING A FRIEND

By the time Greg Pacynski came to his third church, he was ready for major responsibility. He had proven himself in teen work and was now minister of Christian education at a large church in Birmingham. This put him in charge of all ministry to infants through college age.

High on the list as far as the church was concerned was the need to get the youth department under control. The recent years had seen a rapid turnover of youth pastors. Greg looked at the salary allocation for this post and thought he saw part of the problem already. But he determined to make do with what was authorized.

He and a search committee went to work. Their first choice was a graduate student who served well for six months but then left to pursue a doctorate.

The second youth pastor looked good on paper but soon revealed fatal flaws. Brian Lovell was stiff in front of a group; he almost seemed not to like kids. "I knew at the end of the first week we were in trouble," says Greg, "and the church board was going to say, 'Same old revolving door,' before long." When he tried to coach Brian, the man would nod agreement but then proceed on an opposite track. The youth group began to shrink precipitously. Brian's quick explanation: lack of parental support.

Brian and Jolene lived only two blocks from Greg and Kara, and the two staff wives became close friends. Says Kara:

> She became pregnant not long after they arrived, and I kind of took her under wing, helping her choose an obstetrician and get started making plans. We were back and forth for coffee a lot.
>
> But as the trouble began to build at the church, I began to hear more and more sob stories. Our relationship went into a chill, because here I was the wife of her husband's immediate boss! It was hard for me to support Greg sometimes. He'd come home, and I'd jump on him about what Jolene had said—only to find out there was more to the tale than I'd heard.

Within six months, Brian's performance had come before the church board for discussion.

Unfortunately, the senior pastor was at that point locked in a serious power struggle with the board chairman. The two combatants, however, came to a rare consensus in this case: Brian was not cut out to be a youth pastor and ought to be terminated. The board concurred.

On a Tuesday, Greg gathered his courage and called Brian into his office to carry out the decision. It did not go well. Brian strongly objected, became angry, accused Greg and the church of misleading him, of not supporting him, of making him a scapegoat. Both men went home in knots.

The next day, Kara phoned her erstwhile friend to express her personal concern. Jolene spat out one sentence: "I just really think the whole thing is unfair, and I can't talk about it now." She hung up.

The following day, Kara tried again. This time she got a longer recitation of the Lovells' case against the church. The conversation lasted maybe fifteen minutes but left the two women still at odds.

Greg and Kara felt badly enough as it was, but when he mentioned that the board had decided to hold a special meeting of teens and parents following the Sunday evening service to explain what had happened—and *he* would be the moderator—Kara began to worry.

I supported the decision to let Brian go; on that we were agreed. But drag it out in front of everybody in a public meeting? Something inside me said, *Oh, no!* That was just asking for trouble.

At the meeting of two hundred teens and parents, Kara sat in the back, fidgeting. Greg announced the subject for the night and then called on the senior pastor to make the official statement. The tension inside Kara began to throb; she couldn't bear to stay. So she slipped out, collected her children from the nursery, and drove home praying.

Once the floor was opened for questions, a nasty scene ensued. Before it was over, charges and countercharges flew through the air. The matter became embroiled in the larger struggle going on in the church, and Greg found himself trying to referee a shouting match. The meeting attenders did not so much adjourn as simply retreat to let the air clear and count the wounded.

Late that night, Greg finally came through the front door of his home, a beaten man. He took one look at Kara. The words came out slowly: "We have a royal mess on our hands. This may be our Waterloo." His wife's misgivings about the public meeting had proved all too prescient. His attempts at playing church diplomat had come to ashes.

Kara resisted the urge to say, "I told you so." By a week later, things had moderated considerably. The senior pastor had thought better of his outburst at the meeting and apologized. The chairman of the board, seeing that the pastor was recovering his base of support, resigned his post and left the church. As for Greg, his failure to stabilize the youth ministry up to now went undiscussed amid the larger fireworks.

His third choice as youth pastor ended up staying three years and doing a fine job with the teens. Upset parents gradually came back to affirm Greg's leadership and the hard decision he had helped make. Greg and Kara breathed easier with every passing month.

Nevertheless, the husband's role in this church skirmish ended up not only separating pastoral colleagues but costing the wife a friendship. This naturally made her question the judgments of her husband, his superiors, and the church. Kara managed to support Greg throughout, but not without pain.

> I finally came to peace when I was willing to say, "God, you've put Greg in this place of leadership. He's my husband. I'll give input as it seems appropriate but leave the final decisions up to him, knowing I cannot protect him from hurt."
>
> To this day I am thankful for what that ordeal taught me.

REFLECTIONS
by Louis McBurney

The stress of church politics is bound to come sooner or later in a ministry marriage. Thus, it is important to learn conflict management techniques ahead of time, how to get the opposing parties together, how to recognize and realize what's happening on a feeling level with people, how to look at options and bring some resolution. We have to admit that simply praying together, good as that is, doesn't always solve the problem. It can help a lot, but sometimes you need negotiation skills, too.

It would have been good if Brian Lovell could have been offered what the Alban Institute calls "outplacement service." Rather than just approaching him punitively, it would have been good to offer some options and help him find a place to minister more comfortably.

When a person feels locked into a narrow interpretation of call, a lot of options fall by the wayside. I personally hold a very broad definition and try to help people see they can be centered in God's will doing a lot of different things, even "secular" jobs.

The church world is sometimes terribly dishonest in this area. Young ministers tell me about being called into a meeting for this announcement: "Look—you're not making it in this church. We won't say anything public; we'll just give you six months to find another church." So the guy moves along with his problems!

We really can do much better in this area.

So often the minister's wife feels isolated in a church. In a large church with a multiple staff, it's good for wives to help and support one another. But in this case, it turned out to create a secondary problem.

Nevertheless, we must still recognize the need for friends. A lot of ministerial wives feel that's dangerous; they're even told in seminary, "Don't get close to anybody; it only creates problems." Actually, isolation creates as many problems as does friendship.

The friend doesn't have to be somebody in the church body, if that would create a social or political problem. But a listening ear is essential.

ELEVEN

The McKnights:
THE EXPERIMENT
THAT FAILED

Four years after the McKnights came
to Dearborn, Michigan (see chapter 8), they accepted a position that sounded ideal to them: co-pastor of 2,000-mem-
ber Trinity Lutheran Church in Amarillo, Texas. Jerry was
now forty-two, Arlene was forty, and two of their three children were on their own or in college. The southwestern climate and lifestyle attracted them, but even more exciting was
the chance to work with Ray Gundry.

Jerry had met him through a denominational commission
and greatly respected the strong church he had built over the
past fifteen years. The more Ray talked about Jerry becoming
his partner in ministry, sharing the vision, and regular
preaching, the more the McKnights paid attention. The
chance to preach 40 percent of the time was especially
attractive.

Several of their friends questioned whether a bipolar leadership structure would work, but others gave it a green light.

Actually, there remains a difference even today about the
term *co-pastor*. Jerry says that was the bargain; Ray says not
quite. Both men recognized that Ray, by virtue of his long
service in Amarillo, would continue to be the de facto leader of

the church. They wanted some title for Jerry that reflected a shared ministry, so in the end they agreed to drop all adjectives and just be "Pastor Gundry," "Pastor McKnight."

It turned into a nightmare.

Says Ray:

> I wasn't aware, I guess, of how I came across to Jerry. What I thought was helpful instruction on my part—background information—he viewed as paternalistic. I had said, "I want to willingly share the ministry with you, so long as I have 51 percent of the vote." He thought that meant 51 percent of the *decisions*. There's a difference.
>
> I thought I was secure enough to let titles go. But I never saw myself as a "co-pastor."

Jerry remembers a couple of times the first year when he failed to acknowledge Ray's prominence in the denomination, and Ray reacted sharply. After times like that, Jerry began thinking about the eight-thousand-dollar cut in salary he had taken to come to Amarillo. He reserved most of his strong speeches, however, for Arlene.

> One day Jerry came home and said, "I don't know; we may not be staying here."
>
> I just came apart. "Oh, no! I can't bear to move again."
>
> By this time, we'd probably moved ten times in our married life, and I was tired of it. I was just starting to get settled. I had some good friends.
>
> My personality is such that I've always dreamed of being in one place—forever! Maybe I should have lived a hundred years ago. My sister's husband works an eight-to-five job at General Motors. They've lived in one house all their lives. I'd end up talking about that when Jerry would come home frustrated.

At the end of the second year, the two pastors went on a personal retreat. Jerry expressed his feeling that the dream was not really working and that he should start looking elsewhere. Ray's response: "While that is not what I want, I agree it would probably be in the best interest of both of us."

That word was gradually spread to the board chairman, then the whole board, and finally the membership. The McKnights sold their home and rented a condominium while Jerry began setting up candidating trips to other churches. The board, however, asked Jerry to stay on, and after other options did not develop, he said he would. The McKnights took a deep breath and bought another house.

By this time, some in the congregation were developing a deep affinity for Jerry. He was asked at one point to conduct the funeral of a retired minister in the congregation, and when he gently said to the widow, "Wouldn't you like to have Pastor Gundry conduct the service?" she said no. Ray said nothing directly about the matter, but his reaction showed itself in a different direction: an angry exchange with the principal of the church's parochial school, whom Jerry had recruited and was currently trying to defend against charges of incompetence.

The McKnights stayed another three years in Amarillo, five in all, and the details of the struggle vary depending on who is being interviewed. Suffice it to say that by the end, both men were depleted. Jerry and Arlene moved to a senior pastorate back in their native Canada.

By that time, they had spent many a lunch together talking about what to do. Arlene would rebuff talk of relocation, reminding Jerry how often they had moved in the past. Jerry would rebut that by saying, "But didn't we sense God's direction each time? Which of the moves do you think we shouldn't have made?" His wife would agree that she had concurred with each change. Says Jerry:

> Each of us used leverage on the other, I guess. I'd push the spiritual angle, and she'd talk about the need for stability, the trouble we had with our son last move, and how she hated to leave her friends.
>
> She also feared becoming *the* senior pastor's wife; she enjoyed being in the shadows as just one of the staff.

I admit, when I go into a new situation, it has built-in potential for relationships: a new board, new staff, the membership, all looking my direction. Rapport comes easily. That's not the case with a wife; she's more on her own in a strange place.

More often, though, Arlene listened thoughtfully to her husband and tried to help him cope.

It was sad for us all. I hurt for Jerry, because I could see how he was upset. I hurt for *me,* because I'd hoped it was going to be a really terrific experience, and it wasn't.

The truth is, both Jerry and Arlene have done well in their new location. They are happy, and their church is launching an energetic building program. Ray Gundry is not surprised:

Jerry needed to be on his own—God put that capacity into his life. Naturally, I would say his years here helped get him ready for the larger responsibility. I don't know if he would see it that way.

From this church's point of view, however, it was a great experiment that didn't work. In fact, it was an injustice to Jerry. One pastor has to be ultimately responsible in a church.

I made plenty of mistakes, I know; I wasn't lily-white in all that happened. I made some wrong assumptions about Jerry. The truth is, those were the toughest years of my ministry. They produced the greatest stress even on *my* marriage.

The two men have had almost no contact since the McKnights left. Jerry, however, still asserts that Ray Gundry's heart is good, his intentions honorable, in spite of the deadlock that evolved. He also has gained some objectivity about his own role:

From a human point of view, it was a terrible experience. The whole thing was stupid. But looking at it as a Christian, I believe God has his hand in our lives and directs our steps. So although it was a tough time, we made it through, and I learned a lot.

REFLECTIONS
by Louis McBurney

This is a dramatic case of expectations not being synchronized. Amarillo looked like a dream situation to the McKnights, and they entered without evaluating closely enough what was likely to happen. We could wish Ray and Jerry had asked questions such as "What do you imagine it will be like as co-pastors? What do you envision will be your area of involvement? What does having 51 percent of the vote mean?" (That was a crucial point.)

Church staff design is, admittedly, a real challenge, because so many of the issues do *not* show up until after the honeymoon. You can, however, decrease the intensity of the problems by establishing good communication patterns right away, during the honeymoon, by learning to sit down and talk together about what's going on in the relationship between pastors. That way, when the problems come along, you'll be able to cope with them more effectively.

About the most positive thing that happened was when the two men retreated. At least they made an attempt to talk it out.

However, they were not successful in the long run. This raises the implications of disagreement. Because of our own personal needs or insecurities, we often enter conflict situations with a win-lose approach. If you happen to have a strong need to win, you draw firm lines, and you *can't* just disagree. Unless the other person concedes, you feel you lost.

Theologically, God always wins and the Devil loses, right? So when two godly men disagree about something, the Devil must be in one of them!?

But if you look at Scripture, you see example after example of people losing, not making their point, disagreeing. And if you really take seriously Christ's teaching about going the second mile or turning the other cheek, it is hard to insist on winning all the time.

The reason a person isn't able to back off is that he has his own worth or survival tied up with always being right. This betrays a basic lack of trust in God's ability to work. It also flies in the face of Jesus' teaching about judgmentalism. Often when you feel you must win, you have to judge the other person as wrong, not just different.

Some things don't need to be settled *today*. Some things don't need to be settled ever. Others, however, may require you to say, "You know, this is a point I don't think we're ever going to agree on. Can we have a relationship anyway?" Maybe you can, maybe you can't.

But often if you stop to analyze, *Why is this so important to me?* you will diffuse the need to make the other person see it your way. Some of these things come simply with age, living long enough to see the eternal perspective.

TWELVE

Joe Keysor:
PART OF THE
FAMILY PACKAGE?

A serious problem is planted in the pastoral home when the children living there do not actually embrace the faith for themselves but simply fulfill a role. Their quiet conformity is mistaken for genuine commitment. But the pretending will not last forever.

Chuck and Marge Keysor,* who now serve Countryside Evangelical Covenant Church in Clearwater, Florida, have finished raising their five children. Chuck is an articulate, ambitious man, the kind of person you'd expect to find in an advertising agency, which is where he started out after journalism school. Later on, he gave up his agnosticism at a Billy Graham crusade and, in 1963, entered seminary. His oldest child was thirteen, his youngest four when he became student pastor of a church in Elgin, Illinois.

His wife is much quieter, the daughter of Finnish immigrants, who tends to think a long time before speaking. She is a good ballast for her energetic husband.

Both of them, however, plunged into the work of their

---

* This is the sole vignette in this book where actual names and places are used, since part of the Keysors' story has already been published.

parish with dedication and swept their children along in the tide. Sunday school, youth groups, and other church events were standard fixtures in the weekly schedule.

Joe, the second-born, left for college in 1970. Four years later, he had his degree but no plan of action; he spent a year drifting around the country. He finally landed back home with Mom and Dad, who had since moved to teach at a Christian college.

In Chuck's book *Forgiveness Is a Two-Way Street,* he writes about the night everything came unraveled:

> We were having supper on Christmas Eve. My wife and I were seated with four of our five children and my wife's father round the table. The table was decorated with festive candles. Red, blue, yellow, and green lights beamed on the family Christmas tree and piles of presents lay underneath. . . . The spicy smell of baked ham filled the house; all was in order for a Christmas both holy and merry.
>
> After dinner I took my Bible and opened to the Christmas story in Luke. Reading this familiar passage on Christmas Eve was an established part of our family tradition. As I opened the Bible, Joe . . . suddenly got up from the table and left the dining room. His abrupt departure created a sense of shock and a cloud descended over our Christmas Eve. The scowl on Joe's face had made it plain that he was annoyed about something.
>
> "I guess he doesn't feel well," I said lamely. After an awkward pause I began to read, "And it came to pass in those days . . ." We lingered at the table, talking about other things. But the cloud was still there and so was Joe's empty chair. I wondered, *What on earth is the matter with him?*
>
> Later that evening when he and I were alone together in the living room, I could see in his eyes that something was smoldering.
>
> "Joe," I finally asked, "what is wrong?"
>
> What followed was an hour of the most honest conversation I had ever had with my son. . . .
>
> "You always just *assumed* that I believed everything," he said bitterly. "I was a part of the family's religion. I don't want to go along with that charade any more! Tonight I decided to be honest.

So I got up and left the table before you read from the Bible. I didn't want to sit there and *pretend* that I believe all that stuff."

In line with her quiet nature, Marge was not present for all this. She had, in fact, gone on to bed after the long day. "I didn't understand what had happened," she says, "and I'm not a person who reacts quickly. I guess I'm more of a Finn than I realize. I tend to think, 'Well, let's wait and see what happens.' "

Meanwhile, Chuck laid himself open by asking such things as "What's really happening to us? What did your leaving the table represent?" Inwardly he prayed for the strength not to lecture. He writes:

> Our conversation was like peeling back the layers of an onion. Tears came to my eyes as layer after layer of my son's frustration and suppressed indignation were exposed. Things from long ago—things I could only dimly remember—came alive again as part of the ugly litany, resurrecting my numerous failures as a father.
>
> Joe also hinted at some very personal things that had happened to him during college—things his mother and I had prayed would *not* happen. . . . At last I was beginning to understand my son.
>
> His verbal assault had a strange effect on me. I was praying that I might really hear him. . . . Yet as the recitation continued, I felt dismayed. . . . A desperate feeling of failure began to rise within me. And guilt! . . .
>
> Why do I share this personal experience of one of the most unpleasant hours of my life? Because it illustrates a keystone principle of family life: *It is often the darkest just before the dawn.* As the psalmist wrote, "Weeping may last for the night, but a shout of joy comes in the morning" (Ps. 30:5).
>
> Raising five children to adulthood, my wife and I have learned that God may be most creatively at work in our times of deepest despair and failure.

As the Keysor household moved into the new year, a gradual change began to occur. Communication with Joe improved slowly, often during the times Chuck would make for doing things together—playing Scrabble, lingering over lunch, going fishing—"little things." The talk was superficial at first, but eventually it deepened as Joe realized his parents sincerely wanted to listen, not chastise.

"I began to comprehend that the most important things in life are relational, not intellectual," says Chuck.

> Rebuilding the bridge between us took several years. By God's grace we all learned to be more patient with each other—even when our viewpoints clashed. . . .
>
> Church presented a prickly problem. . . . Again, the Holy Spirit took charge. He gave us the right words and spirit. As I remember, I said something like this to our son: "Joe, the things of God are most important to your mother and me. For us to be honest and natural, we have to say this. But you are an adult and it is not our responsibility to drag you to church. You are responsible directly to God and I believe that in His own time and way, He will create within you a desire. Then you'll want to be with God's people."
>
> We left it at that and went to church by ourselves.
>
> . . . One Sunday as we ate our meal, he mentioned the morning service. So we knew that he had chosen to attend. Probably he sat by himself up in the church balcony.
>
> Our conversation naturally moved into the sermon. And we realized Joe had indeed "gotten the message." This began to happen regularly.

On Easter afternoon, Joe finally told his parents he had realized his need for Christ and made a commitment to follow him. As Chuck and Marge tried to contain their joy, their son suggested the family should study the Bible and pray together from now on. They had come full circle.

> God, in His wisdom and perfect timing, did what Joe's mother and I could not do: He made our son a Christian. In retrospect we could discern the Lord's hand in the very restlessness and dead ends which had brought our son home again. We realized that

God had been at work even in the disruption of our family, in the deep resentment and painful alienation.

With Joe's permission I have shared this episode of our personal family history. God can still work miracles in the family circle. His grace *can* erase all the horrendous mistakes.[1]

One of those mistakes, Chuck now sees, was the common problem of a too-full agenda in the pastorate. The idea of taking a day off seemed impractical at the time. "I admit I allowed my work to intrude," he says. "That's easy for someone in Christian work. If you're conscientious, you see the needs, and you move in, as into a vacuum. But you pay a price for that, and it's not always a good bargain. Much of what happened ten and twenty years ago in my ministry is dross. But the relationship with my kids is irreplaceable.

"It takes a certain maturity to realize you're in the kind of task where, even if you were triplets working twenty-four hours a day, you still wouldn't get done. I'm not advocating complacency or goofing off. But you shouldn't be driven, either. Holiness and godliness are not the same as working yourself to a frazzle."

His unflappable wife adds a bit of sage wisdom: "I guess I think life is a school, and God is teaching us through all these things that bump up against us."

1. Charles Keysor, *Forgiveness Is a Two-Way Street* (Wheaton, Ill.: Victor, 1982), pp. 50–57.

REFLECTIONS:
by Louis McBurney

PKs are an amazing group. They have special grace, I'm convinced; they put up with an awful lot of stress and abuse from congregations as well as neglect from their minister parent(s). Yet they seem to emerge committed to Christ and understanding the importance of commitment, as this boy did. It's amazing to me how that can happen.

The fact these parents did not know where their son stood is not at all uncommon. Often PKs recognize the tremendous stress and expectations the church puts on their parents, and so they decide just not to cause any additional problems. They go along quietly and keep their own stress inside. (Of course, sometimes there are tremendous examples of the opposite, too! In this story, the implication is that during Joe's college days, he rebelled in ways his parents never knew about and thought he had somehow escaped.)

My wife and I had much the same experience with our older two—and we thought we'd been very perceptive, in-touch parents. Melissa was talking to our oldest son not long ago, who has had a real spiritual renewal in the last year. He had never stopped going to church, but he told his mother he had realized his need to change because, in fact, he had been fairly heavily involved in drugs. He said his body was craving the highs, and he wanted some help with that, so he had really sought Christ.

We knew none of this. A couple of times during high school, he'd gone to a beer bust and come home drunk, but we had no idea he was into more than that. He knew what he was doing would have been very painful for us, so he simply kept quiet, not wanting to hurt us or cause problems.

It is hard to tell a Christian leader, "Don't worry about the social stigma of a wayward child," but I know that the more pressure a child feels to conform, the more intense the rebellion will be. One minister's kid we heard about would get high on pot, then open a parsonage window and yell, "The pastor's wife is a whore!" Well, that gets people's attention!

One of the beautiful things about the Keysor story is that when Joe finally confessed where he was, his father listened to him and accepted him. Often that doesn't happen; the clamps come down, the guilt is thrown on, and the kid is driven away. Joe came back to the belief system of his parents because he was given acceptance and a feeling of being loved; he saw the validity of what they talked about. Rebellious PKs can very often come back to be strong, committed Christians.

Apparently, Joe Keysor felt a degree of openness in his parents' home, the possibility that there *could* be communication. Otherwise, he probably wouldn't have even tried. He would have just left to do his thing somewhere else. But he was comfortable enough in the relationship to risk talking.

THIRTEEN

The Hunters: "DO I NEED AN APPOINTMENT?"

The contrast between Austin and Lois Hunter's first pastorate in the heart of Appalachia and today's upscale Miami congregation is in some ways a parable of the radical shift that overtook their communication.

They spent a little less than two years in Pie, West Virginia, a coal-mining village as homespun as its name, not far from the Kentucky border. This was their internship in the midst of seminary, and they lived in a four-room parsonage, one room of which was Austin's study.

The furnishings were hand-me-downs; plastic curtains hung at all windows. There was no television, no radio, not even a telephone. But most unique was the fact that this house had no interior doors. Each room was open to the other three.

Says Austin with a smile:

> Given the fact that we were newlyweds, that made for its own distractions when I was supposed to be preparing sermons.
>
> Seriously, Lois and I were together more actual hours those first twenty months than most couples are in their first ten years. There was no way to get away from each other! We were practically *never* apart, except when I was out making calls.
>
> It really developed our partnership.

They found out each other's assortment of strengths and gifts in the ministry. They learned how to supplement one another; they discovered where they could work together smoothly and where they were better off taking separate tracks. They look back with fondness to the unity of those early days in the hills.

Once seminary had been completed, the Hunters gave five years to a church in Georgia, where their two children were born. Then came the move to a faltering congregation of fewer than fifty in Miami. They stabilized the ministry there and saw a steady growth begin that has continued for more than fifteen years. Their hearty openness, deep caring, and sincere spirituality has helped attract a congregation of almost a thousand today.

Austin's counseling ministry drew special attention from the beginning. Those who were helped naturally began sending their troubled friends his direction. This, on top of the many other responsibilities of leading a growing church in a metropolitan area, quickly filled his calendar.

Lois was busy herself as a mother, piano teacher, and girls' club director. She did not realize what was happening until sometime in the early 1970s. The church secretary, who worked three days a week, was starting to fall behind, so Lois volunteered to fill in the other two days as a stopgap measure.

A certain woman in the church had a standing appointment with Austin each Tuesday afternoon. For the first time, Lois saw at close range the kind of help and care her husband was extending.

> I knew this gal had a history of emotional problems; it was valid for Austin to be seeing her. But I found myself sitting there at the typewriter crying. I couldn't hear what was being said in the inner office, of course, but I could hear the quiet tone of conversation, the laughter every once in a while—for an hour or even an hour and a half, every week.
>
> I'd try to keep my mind on my typing, but it was tearing my heart out, because I didn't feel even *I* could talk to him an hour and a half a week. I didn't have his undivided attention.

People would drop by the office or stop Lois on Sunday morning to say how wonderful her husband was, how greatly they had been helped by his marvelous caring. That was not what she needed to hear. She wanted to scream back, *Why you and not me?!*

Finally, she decided to speak up. As Austin recalls their encounter:

> In a very firm, no-nonsense way, she said, "Do I have to make an appointment with you in order to receive what I see you giving so generously to others?"
>
> That really rattled my cage. The fact of the matter was, she deserved my time and attention. She should have had it first. Instead, she was getting the leftovers.

That confrontation led to the establishing of a weekly date each Friday from noon to two o'clock, time reserved for the marriage alone. Austin explains the ground rules:

> Lois has control over that time block. She can even cancel it if she wants. But I can't.
>
> She sets the agenda. If she wants me to go shopping with her, fold clothes, work in the yard, read a book out loud, go for a boat ride, go to bed, or whatever . . . here I am. Actually, we've done all those things, and more.
>
> This has become a time I look forward to now. When I fantasize about retirement, I think mainly about spending time with Lois. It's gotten in my blood.

Has this practice solved the deep need for attention and communication in the Hunter marriage? Yes and no. It has created a time-space to look forward to, an assurance that the other person's undivided availability is never more than seven days away. The initials "LH" in Austin's Day-Timer pocket calendar each Friday affirm that here is a priority of the first order.

Lois talks about why it is not a cure-all, however:

Probably my greatest [remaining] frustration is that I can't find time to bring up the tough things that need discussing. I don't want to use my Friday date for those. I don't want to end up in tears then.

I tend to procrastinate on those subjects, keep sweeping them under the rug. But that's not the way to do it.

Still, I find it hard to program my crucial discussions. When something is bothering me on Monday, I can't wait till Friday to talk about it.

Debates in this marriage tend to get noisy, given the two personalities and the homes in which they were raised. Austin, a take-charge kind of man who has been known to chuck his ministerial decorum at a football game and tell an abusive fan to clam up, defends his viewpoint at home as well. It is almost entertaining to listen to this couple describe their face-offs:

AUSTIN: See, I don't like to lose! I don't do anything without intending to win—whether it's foosball, golf, or a formal debate. Otherwise, why mess with it?

Then I get in the car and drive for ten minutes and say, "That was really stupid of me." I need to become more sensitive to the fact that [my aggressiveness] isn't the way to arrive at a decision with someone like Lois.

When I stand up there [in the pulpit] on Sunday, I speak authoritatively. Nobody challenges me—at least not right then. I speak on the veracity of the Word of God, and I *declare* it.

The only problem is, that has a tendency to spill over into private life. I speak authoritatively when I don't have the backing of the Word of God—just my personal opinion!

LOIS: He tends to overpower our arguments. And that devastates me. He regrets it, too, once he realizes it. We've had tears over it—both of us.

AUSTIN: See, if I sense I'm losing an argument, I kick the volume up.

LOIS: Or he'll do what he advises every counselee not to do: he'll grasp for support by bringing up other subjects that are still unresolved.

AUSTIN: If something has been argued *and settled*, we don't bring it up again; that's wrong. But if it's something unresolved, even if unrelated. . . .

For example, Lois has a chronic habit of starting [to prepare for going out] *too late*. At the time I'm ready to leave the house, she's putting a blouse in the dryer. (It's one reason we often drive two cars. I get to the place much less stressed.)

Now, if we get in an argument about whether we're going to make a certain purchase, or something about the children—I've been known to say, "You're angry because the kids are indifferent to time. Well, you *trained* them to be that way!" It has nothing to do with the subject at hand, but it sure helps the argument.

My points are always valid; they're just not always relevant! [Laughter from Lois]

We don't have major disagreements. We have major flare-ups over minor disagreements.

LOIS: But he has mellowed through the years. He's had to work at it. His whole family is very explosive. Now, whenever we go see his brother on vacation, he can't get over how bossy he is to his wife.

AUSTIN: In our twenty-seven years of marriage, I have accomplished a great deal in that I've taught Lois how to fight. I've created a monster for myself, but. . . .

She didn't know how to deal with conflict. Now she can confront it.

When we first married, I could blow her out of the water with the first four-cylinder word. I *knew* she didn't understand some of the words, 'cause I made 'em up! Now, she knows who she is and where she's coming from. She values herself. She's more than just Austin Hunter's wife.

How has this couple come to such a freewheeling and yet healthy relationship? One senses a great deal of positive respect and love between them. Perhaps the Friday dates have something to do with that. These people know they are important to each other, important enough to turn off the world, the ministry, and the children at least once a week. From this base has grown wholeness and strength.

REFLECTIONS
by Louis McBurney

The closeness Lois sees her husband having with other people creates several feelings: neglect, loneliness, anger, and insecurity about herself as a person, wondering what she's done or hasn't done that makes her somehow undeserving.

This is common among ministers' wives. What often happens is that the wife becomes increasingly hostile and critical about the situation, which only drives her husband further away.

It is important for pastors and wives to realize that the dynamics of church relationships are very different from the husband/wife relationship. It is extremely easy for a woman in the church to see him as a hero. When that happens, the pastor can begin to operate according to Willie Sutton's Law ("I rob banks 'cause that's where the money is"). He spends time where he gets acclaim, praise, and good strokes.

It is striking in this narrative how Lois grew as a person after the beginning of the Friday date, how she began to speak up to Austin more. She is now more than just the pastor's wife, says her husband; she knows who she is. It is crucial for wives to develop a sense of identity for themselves. As they become more secure in themselves as persons of worth and value, apart from their husbands, they are able to deal more effectively with conflict in the relationship as well as in the church.

Some women have trouble taking the initiative as Lois Hunter did. My suggestion is that they go and talk with an older, mature Christian woman who can listen and can tell her own life experience. They may be threatened by the prospect of going to a professional counselor, but they can feel comfortable approaching another pastor's wife or someone similar.

There are any number of good books about self-esteem that are helpful, too.

Ultimately, it's good if the husband can get involved in this development of his wife's self-identity. We find it extremely valuable to include the spouse in our counseling, so that whatever is dealt with and learned is reinforced at home rather than sabotaged—which is what often happens when one person goes away, gets some insight, and tries to change.

Wives sometimes have to be willing to yell and get some attention, as Lois Hunter did. They have to point out their need. We've heard of wives who have called their husband's office and, using a pseudonym, made an appointment to see him! Anything like that is fair game to get the attention of a workaholic.

FOURTEEN

The Owenses:
FAST-TRACK PASTORING

T he difference between David and Jackie Owens's first church—the two excruciating years in Tennessee (chapter 3)—and the second church in Van Wert, Ohio, was the difference between a stagnant situation and one with growth potential. As the couple adjusted to the realities of pastoring, David began to thrive in the ministry, and the rise in attendance figures paralleled the boost in his own spirit. He still had to work part-time in order to support the family, but his love affair with the pastorate blossomed regardless. He remains infatuated to this day.

> I find myself too often having early meetings. I like to meet with a new Christian or a potential Christian, maybe a business person, and catch breakfast before they go to work at eight. And the day just keeps going from there.
>
> Even when I'm bushed, I guess I just love the work of God. Roll me out of bed, point me in the direction of the shower, and I'll head [automatically] for the restaurant.
>
> I don't drag and mope and grumble, "Oh, I hate this." I love it.

In Van Wert, the idea of taking a day off was preposterous to David, given the challenge of the church and also the need to work an extra job. The more Jackie began to get her bearings as a pastor's wife, the more she began to notice his absence.

> I thoroughly enjoyed the fact that I could be home with the children. But Saturdays were extremely hard for me, because everybody else's husband was home that day. Families were together.
>
> Saturday was the day I didn't see David all day. He was in the office preparing, and I would be home with not a lot to do.

One particular weekend stands out in her memory. A special Friday evening dinner was planned; Jackie cannot remember now, twenty years later, whether company had been invited or whether it was to be romantic candlelight for just the two of them. She does recall setting the table with her best dishes and preparing a menu to impress.

Suddenly David came across the street from the church. He had to leave right away for an overnight trip to Cleveland with someone. He'd be back late the next day.

Both David and Jackie have by now forgotten the particulars of this trip and whether it was truly urgent or not. They still recall the feelings it triggered, however. Says Jackie:

> I was so angry. Once again, his choice was somebody else.
>
> In *his* mind, it had nothing to do with his love for me or wanting to be with me. But in my mind, it had everything to do with that. I wasn't important.

By the time David returned Saturday evening, Jackie was deep into silence. The next morning, they went to church and performed as expected, but at the Sunday dinner table, the only sounds came from children and utensils.

Finally, David decided to get to the bottom of this. "Why are you acting this way?" he asked. "Why don't you talk to us?"

Jackie could manage no words. Seven years of occupying second place in her husband's life finally exploded. She grabbed a table knife and flung it backwards across the bare floor. Two little girls looked up wide-eyed as their mother stormed from the room.

David took a deep breath, then excused himself and followed his wife into the bedroom. "Jackie, please tell me what's wrong."

She could only stare at him, then turn away.

> I knew the way I was acting wasn't right, but I was so hurt . . . I felt he'd been so unfair. The thing had just been getting bigger and bigger inside of me.
>
> I mentally packed my bags more than once those days. I knew he loved me, and I thought if I left, he would really be in trouble. I mean, he just wouldn't be able to stand it! That would be my way of hurting him back.

Would she take the children? No—but then how could she get along without them? What would she use for money? That was a major problem. Where would she go? She didn't know.

Her fantasy was impractical, she admitted, but that did not stop her from reconsidering it several times. Three weeks went by with the relationship deeply frozen. Then came a week of special meetings at the church with a white-haired Bible teacher named Foster Mathewson. He stayed, of course, at the parsonage.

> After church the second night, we were sitting at the table having coffee and refreshments, and he looked up at David and said, "Is your wife always this quiet, or is something wrong?"
>
> I was just floored. I thought, *Oh, my goodness.* I looked at him, and I looked at David, and David looked at me and said, "Well, would you like to answer?"
>
> I finally said, "Well, I'm not always this quiet." I didn't know what else to say.

The older man began to talk. In a kindly but direct way he said, "I think, my dear, you have been going on your reserves for quite a long time, and you are close to running out. The Lord does not want either of you to live this way." He counseled them both not to hold back from each other but to give one another the time and attention a godly marriage needs. Jackie dissolved in tears.

> That whole week of meetings was really just for David and me, more than anyone else in the church. We prayed, and that was the beginning of my relief.
> Not long after that we left Van Wert.

When, after fifteen months away from the pastorate (David traveled as an evangelist and Jackie stayed with the children back in Tennessee), they began their church ministry in Phoenix, the board strongly urged a pastoral day off. "Take the phone off the hook," they said. "If anyone really needs you, they'll come to the door."

David tried Mondays at first, realized he was too drained to be much good, and so switched to Fridays. He and Jackie later bought a mountain cabin away from the city in order to have a hideaway. Whenever the subject turns to his personal life, he is openly apologetic about his early priorities.

> I *have* neglected family; there's just no way I can excuse it or justify it. I'm afraid I've always been one to say, "Next week, it's going to be better. There will be more time for the family." And that usually hasn't come off.
> I'm deeply grateful for the way Jackie has somehow been able to develop ministries for herself without sitting around and moping. That has filled some of the inner vacuum in times when I was not giving. And she's never turned the kids away from God, or the church, or me. They *love* the church; they love God; they even love me. It's *unreal*, because she really got shortchanged.

Now that the children are grown, David and Jackie do not get to the mountains as frequently, and when they do, she finds him with his nose in a book too much for her liking. She is not beyond occasionally telling David he should have been a priest. They laugh together at the crack, but both know there's a meaning underneath.

David fights to make room in his Day-Timer for staying home. But he loses as often as he wins. Like Jeremiah, there is a fire in his bones:

> Look at all this population. We're in the capital city, with a university to boot. How many churches are even making a dent?
>
> We're doing better in one sense than we've ever done, and I don't disparage what God is doing and has done. As a matter of fact, our church is one of the strongest in town, in the county. But what's a thousand people in more than half a million?
>
> I'm not just talking about a numbers game, a pride and ego thing. We've got all this wide-open opportunity here: it's an intellectual city, it's a professional city—dear God!
>
> I know you win people to Christ one by one. But still, I am so *frustrated!* I say, "What's the next step, Lord? What's the key?" He's helped us year by year; now we have the building and the acreage. We can go to three services with twelve hundred in a service; that means we could have a thirty-six hundred morning attendance without having to build again. . . .

He says all this not in weariness but with a light in his eye, a forward tilt to his body. This is *fun.* This is *living.* Eighty-hour weeks—so what? He will make the most of his calling and gifts not out of duty but because he can imagine no greater thrill.

Meanwhile, Jackie watches . . . and waits.

> I am a person who needs to talk things out. And David just doesn't have time. It's "catch me when you can."
>
> He'll say, "Tomorrow morning I'll stay home a little while longer, and we'll have coffee and talk." That just excites me no end!
>
> But it absolutely never works out. We barely get into a conversation, and the phone rings, and he's off . . . or somebody comes to the door, or he remembers something he's got to write down. In my mind, I think, *This shouldn't bother me so much.* But it does.

Jackie has discovered over the years almost a perverse coincidence: Her times of greatest need seem to hit when David is busiest. The church has just bought a camp, or it's time to reorganize the Christian education program, or a great opportunity has just come for David to visit a foreign mission site . . . all legitimate things, but hard to applaud when you're craving quiet togetherness.

She has created her own outlets, of course; the same verve that made her a maverick in the early days helps her stay busy today. In spite of their busy pace, she and David maintain a positive atmosphere; their children, now grown, are sources of common joy. Among the common projects are team teaching and occasional joint counseling at the church.

But the sore spot of time alone remains. It is sore enough now that Jackie has come to resent the two-birds-with-one-stone approach:

> The time David sets aside for us is always intertwined with something else in the ministry. He's going to a conference, so why don't I go along and we can talk on the way. It's never open-ended. It's never "Let's go away for the day just us."
>
> I feel like I'm always being pushed into the Day-Timer; *We're going to get Jackie in here somewhere.*
>
> I know that's *not* his attitude, but that's what I have to deal with.

When Jackie turns cold from waiting too long, David quickly realizes it. He immediately feels guilty, pulls out his calendar—and realizes he is locked in for the next three weeks. To break away before next month is not just difficult; it is impossible.

In recent years he has sometimes found himself reforming too late: he has invited Jackie to a time away only to find *her* calendar booked. She has a women's Bible study to lead, or she's scheduled to have lunch with a counselee, or it's time to start planning the fall missions banquet.

Is there a danger that two separate tracks will develop in this marriage, especially now that the empty-nest years have come? David responds:

Yes, it's possible. She has developed such a ministry here that she doesn't realize it's not always me who has the problem.

We're like a two-career marriage, undoubtedly. And if we do not come back and re-establish our commitment and time and tender loving care regularly, then I suppose we could go our separate ways, and pretty soon, we'd be to the place of who needs each other? We're very mindful of that.

David and Jackie Owens will most likely hold their marriage together in years to come, if for no other reason than that they will have to slow down. They also have the legacy of weathering a great number of other storms in the past. Their common love for the church will keep their paths crossing even when they are too busy to plan for it. Neither one *dislikes* the pastorate. Neither can think, at this stage, of doing anything else.

But it is fortunate that they were born in a generation that was taught the permanence of marriage. A younger couple might not be so resolute. The Owens marriage is held together by its formal commitment even on days when the partners neglect to nurture its essence. Says Jackie:

One thing I do know is [the time frustration] has nothing to do with how much he loves me or cares for me. There's not a doubt in my mind about that. It's just that we need to keep working through this.

REFLECTIONS
by Louis McBurney

Again, a busy pastorate.

One of the things that strikes me about the early days of this ministry marriage is the lack of support, the isolation. It took the visiting evangelist to identify the problem at home and minister to David and Jackie. That is a common story. I've known a number of evangelists who have said their ministry is as much with the pastors they visit as the congregations they preach to. It's sad that so many ministers feel they cannot talk with someone about the problems they're having.

These two people have developed separate interests. That can be either divisive or enriching. Floyd and Harriett Thatcher's book *Long-Term Marriage* (Word, 1980) deals with this effectively. Many churches need education about this, especially if they have a stereotypic role for the pastor's wife to play, and if they create problems and tensions for her when she steps outside that role.

A key to keeping a separate interest from being divisive is sharing it with one another. By bringing it back into the relationship, it becomes enriching. But if you tend to do your own thing and never bring it home, the result is likely to be division.

Jackie Owens knows her husband's love. Regardless of the fact that he's too busy some of the time, she still has a foundation: he loves her, and he's special to her. When that is in place, some of the other things lose their impact. When it's not in place, most anything can rock the boat.

The idea of a wife being important and number one is communicated in lots of ways, positively and negatively. Part of it is time together, but other parts are the respect a husband shows for what she says, whether he asks her opinion about things, how much of himself he shares with her. All these are positive signals to a woman.

Another part of this case deals with play, something a lot of ministers have never been able to do. They either have a high sense of responsibility, which is why they're in ministry, or they're workaholics needing to prove themselves. Either trap prevents a person from learning to relax and enjoy life. Even the leisure activities of these men become highly competitive; they must win.

This inner drive probably saps a man's joy more than even church demands or church stress. Most churches are now willing and even eager for their pastors to take the personal space they need. The only remaining question is whether the pastor himself will get in touch with his inner motivations and be willing to be freed up.

When David Owens says he just loves getting up in the morning and heading for the work of the ministry, he doesn't sound like a man driven by a tremendous inner need to prove himself. He simply enjoys what he does. And that's fine.

But there is another consideration: he has a wife, and she has legitimate needs, too. He can't always do what he enjoys doing most.

Part Three
PERSONAL STRESSES

The hazards of the previous section, though intensely personal and close-range, are still "objective" to a degree. They can be named, analyzed, compartmentalized.

The personal stresses to which we turn now are more internal, less organized, more amorphous. They are harder to "blame on the church." They are the vexations of soul, the plagues that strike at self-definition, self-respect, security.

Some of the ministry couples in the following pages talk about their struggles to define roles, to focus the contribution each has to make. Some deal with aloneness in the ministry. Some portray communication problems, getting beyond small talk to deep communion. Then, three separate case histories present the difficult subjects of temptation and unfaithfulness.

Among the many definitions of love over the centuries, here is one with a bite to it: Love is giving someone your undivided attention. *Wives need that. Husbands need that. More than one pastor who has come to realize the limits of sermons and meetings craves a deep fellowship with just one other person. His wife? Sometimes she is too busy mothering, leading the church women's organization, or working at a secular job. This situation, of course, is not nearly as frequent as the opposite case: a preoccupied husband and a deprived wife. But both cases are hard to bear. And both are dangerous.*

As in the other sections of this book, each vignette is followed by

"Reflections." This time the source is David Seamands, longtime United Methodist missionary, then pastor, author, and now associate professor of pastoral ministries at Asbury Theological Seminary, Wilmore, Kentucky.

FIFTEEN

The Pacynskis:
TURNING THE
TABLES

For Greg and Kara Pacynski, neither the early hospitalization (chapter 5) nor the messy firing of a staff associate (chapter 10) were as troubling to their marriage as their struggle over a number of years with identity. For one thing, both of the other situations were fairly short-term; a few months, and life was back to normal. But defining roles and contributions has taken longer to settle.

In the early days of youth ministry, before children came along, Kara did nearly everything with her husband. There were occasional moments when she felt shut out, when Greg was too busy to notice her, but most of the time (after conquering the kidney infection) she was in the swirl of action along with him.

Ryan's arrival, after five years of marriage, coincided in some ways with Greg's ascension as a youth leader of note. Attendance was swelling, the group was winning awards at regional gatherings, the church board of elders was impressed. Two weeks after Ryan's birth, for example, was youth camp.

At the last minute, Kara came down sick with a breast infection. Well—I *had* to go to camp; that was all there was to it. I stashed her with the senior pastor and his wife for good, loving care, while I headed out to save the world of kids.

In my mind, I wasn't abandoning her; she'd be with a woman she loved who would take care of everything. So no big deal, right?

To Kara, it *was* a big deal. She felt deserted with a newborn. But the tape of her father-in-law's warning ("Be careful she doesn't put you on the shelf, Greg") still played in her mind. She was not about to say, "I need you."

The only thing to do was to get back into the stream of ministry as quickly as possible. Soon she was packing Ryan up and toting him to youth retreats, Friday fun nights, basketball games. She continued as much of her public life as she could manage. It was the only way to hold onto Greg, who was now being asked to lead seminars on youth work. The next year he was elected to a term on the denomination's Christian education board.

The summer Ryan turned two provided a watershed moment. They were on a mission trip to Mexico: Greg, Kara, a third adult sponsor, and a dozen teenagers. They arrived to find that the missionary and the national church had not followed through on plans. The work project wasn't ready for them. They had nothing to do. Greg remembers it vividly:

> We got there about four in the morning, after driving straight through from Dallas. Everybody was exhausted and vulnerable. For the first thirty-six hours, the group just basically slept, shopped, and stood around while I—the great "leader" of this expedition—tried to figure out what to do next.
>
> We could go pass out literature on the streets, but if anyone asked a question, we didn't speak Spanish. And they didn't have Mexican young people lined up to be our partners or anything. The whole trip had just kind of stalled out.

Kara, of course, was busy from dawn to nightfall with food preparation for fifteen hungry gringos. She haggled for bargains in the open market, brought the food back to the church, organized kitchen crews, and spent hours over a hot stove. Without her efforts, nobody would have eaten.

Greg recalls the second evening:

> I went to bed around nine o'clock—there was nothing left for me to do. I still didn't have a solution for the next six days. I wanted to talk to Kara about things. But she was still in the kitchen.
>
> I lay there thinking, *Everybody else needs her. They don't need me. Kara, don't you have any time for me? You have time for everybody else, and I'm feeling like a failure down here.*

Kara came to bed around ten, and Greg began to talk. Within minutes, he could see her eyelids beginning to droop. He felt frustrated. "I can't wait till we get home so I can have you again to myself," he said.

Kara opened her eyes wide, looked at him, and delivered one pungent sentence: "Now you know how I've felt all these years."

With that, she rolled over and was soon fast asleep.

Greg was nailed in an instant by the realization that his wife had often felt squeezed out, abandoned, unneeded—the way he felt right then. The temporary role reversal drove her pain home to him. Says Kara:

> That was the beginning of our awareness of the need to talk with each other about how we felt. Seven years of pent-up feeling finally began coming out.
>
> I remember when we got home, we went out to dinner for the express purpose of talking about that night in Monterrey. Greg said, "Now tell me what you meant by that."
>
> And finally—father-in-law or no father-in-law, "shelf" or no "shelf"!—I began talking. For the first time I was able to verbalize, and for the first time he was able to feel.
>
> Our regard for each other didn't turn around overnight, but that was the beginning.

It was good that the breakthrough came when it did, because within two years Ryan had a little sister. That meant a definite trimming of Kara's sails. She recruited another woman in the church to direct the teen plays. The youth newspaper staff tried to do its work around Kara's kitchen table, but that was not always satisfactory.

She did, however, begin to think more about developing her latent interest in writing. At least she could do that at home while the children slept. Greg encouraged her to attend a writers' workshop, and before long she had sold her first article.

About the time Greg turned thirty, he realized he did not want to be a perennial youth man. His reputation in the field meant little to him; he was experiencing some burnout. The move to a larger church as minister of Christian education was an attempt to broaden his scope and recharge his creativity. He found himself, however, with greater desk responsibility. This was not quite his dream for the future, either.

Kara's typewriter kept humming. She was now being *asked* to do articles on assignment. She began work on a master's degree in journalism. Finally, she signed her first book contract.

Greg recalls:

> It was like the success was all in Kara's court. . . . Where was the hero now? What would become of our marriage if I could not be the professional head of the home? Was I really a quality Christian leader or just a pretty face on an overgrown adolescent?
>
> I wasn't all that thrilled about the reputation I'd built. What was I really good for?
>
> There was a movie just then called *A Star Is Born*. Kris Kristofferson was in it—a rock musician who helped his lover—Barbra Streisand—get to the big time as a singer. In the meanwhile, his own career went downhill. I saw a lot of myself in that story. Self-pity, I guess.

What salvaged this situation was the broadened communication that had been constructed in the wake of the Mexico trip. The church also provided for each staff couple a consultation with a Christian psychologist: three tests plus three months of counseling if desired. Greg and Kara welcomed this and learned a great deal about each other in the process. The psychologist pointed out that Greg rated very low in "succorance"—the need to be aided or mothered, while Kara very much wanted to be a caregiver. No wonder they had been tense with each other at times.

The Pacynskis ended up paying their own way for another three months of help and insight. Their relationship has grown and expanded the more they have learned to share feelings and emotions and to affirm the other person's contribution, both professionally and inside the marriage.

REFLECTIONS
by David Seamands

It is my observation that wives—at least in North America—usually begin marriage with a strong desire for intimacy and closeness. Many of them also begin with a low identity of themselves. They don't get much identity fulfillment out of a job, whereas the husband is very much the opposite: he finds great fulfillment in his work and cannot understand his wife's yearnings.

As time goes on, however, these two needs seem to cross. Norman Wright has written that as the man gets older—whether he is a success or a failure—he realizes his job *doesn't* fulfill all his needs. He begins to look for more intimacy and closeness. He becomes more tender toward his wife.

Meanwhile, she is headed the other direction. Her primary work as a mother is now nearing completion, and she begins to seek fulfillment and identity from an outside job. To her husband she says, "Sorry, fella—closeness is what I wanted back yonder, and you didn't give it to me." A lot of marital tragedy takes place right here.

That is why the Mexican debacle was the best thing that ever happened to Greg Pacynski. He learned quickly, only seven years into marriage, that God had made him—and his wife as well—for something bigger than a job, a role.

Kara Pacynski's outburst ("Now you know how I've felt all these years") was excellent; she let him have it. She was very angry and expressed that, but this prevented a long slow burn of repression for years and years. She blew a gasket early, which was very fortunate. It was a shock treatment that forced communication before she developed hardness of heart.

Greg got a taste of his own medicine and saw her pain. He was able to *feel*. That is a strategic ability. In ministry marriages there's a lot of logic/theory/Scripture/ideals stacked up against feeling. Ministers often do not hear their wives' pain.

The breakthrough of communication in this case was really ahead of schedule. Both Greg and Kara made the crossover and began to pay attention to the opposite need (intimacy for the man, identity for the woman), which probably prevented a serious crisis later on. This kind of thing seldom occurs during the twenties. Divorce statistics, we notice, rise noticeably after people have been married sixteen or seventeen years.

When a minister finds too much fulfillment in his work, he doesn't need a spouse—or at least she thinks he doesn't. My wife and I went through a similar crisis that resulted in my finally showing her my weakness. We were in India, and through a converging of nationalism, Hinduism, and communism, we *had* to leave a certain area just as I was drowning in my own successes. We were at the heart of a mass movement; I was baptizing three thousand new believers a year—a rare privilege for a young man in his late twenties. We were building a new church every month. I had said, "This is my dream; we're going to stay here a lifetime." It was a miniature Pentecost.

But God knew better. I would have been the biggest phony in the world if we had stayed there. When we were forced out, I really hit bottom.

Until then, my wife had always seemed a bit on the weepy side, and so I had thought, *My goodness—if I tell her what's bugging me about the church or the mission station—that it's getting to the lonely, scared boy inside of me—we'll both go down the tube together. I don't dare tell her.* I felt I had to play the strong role.

Actually, she *wasn't* weak; she was just expressive. The moment I revealed my weakness, the most amazing thing happened.

She said, "My goodness—I never knew whether you needed me." Suddenly she opened up like a flower to the sun and became the strong person she had always been. I only had to let her know she was needed. I allowed her to minister to me. This met an emotional need in her during a time of life when many wives are tied up with children and can't do much outside. She began a whole new ministry along with me.

The minister who denies his emotional needs is really denying his weaknesses. He thinks he's a ninety-day wonder who can't fail. God has to pull the rug out from under that kind of person.

Oswald Chambers said, "The twin deceivers of the Christian life are success and failure. Christ has not called us to either; he has called us to faithfulness."

SIXTEEN

The Aagards:
HUNGER AND
THIRST

Wayne and JoAnne Aagard, now
in their early fifties, have also been working a long time to
open up their souls to one another. In some ways their current
pastorate at Saint Michael's Presbyterian Church in Yarmouth, Nova Scotia, is a good setting for their personal struggle; the congregation is strong, the Session cooperative, the
two associate ministers competent as well as loyal. Unlike
some of their earlier posts of duty, there are no fires raging in
the membership.

Wayne in some ways is another David Owens (see chapter
14)—handsome, energetic, goal-oriented, at the peak of his
powers, in love with the ministry. Some might even call him
driven. He does not come off that way in public, however; he
moves easily among people, his greetings and stories lighting
up their faces.

JoAnne, on the other hand, is not quite the self-starter
Jackie Owens is. She has carried a running quarrel with the
"pastor's wife" image from the beginning. Her model as a girl
growing up was not positive, and so she did not want to
marry a minister. But she wanted Wayne. She insists she
cannot do the expected things well (play the organ, speak to

groups); hence, the public ministry will never be a full reward for her. Instead, she wants her husband. She wants soul communication. She wants quiet togetherness, not because she has begged for it but because her husband freely arranges it. That is hard for Wayne to remember in the swirl of pastoring.

Underneath this couple's propriety and courtesy to each other, conversation does not flow freely. They tend to sit across the room from each other, not only in the parish hall on social occasions but in their own living room while being interviewed. They weigh their words carefully before responding.

Both agree that in the beginning of their marriage, they could hardly have gotten off to a worse start. Their first year in Toronto was a blur as Wayne, fresh from college, was a youth probation officer and also served as a youth pastor. Both jobs amounted to full-time work, and both supervisors insisted on excellence. He says:

> I don't think I was home three evenings that whole year. And we moved four times. That's real smart!
>
> Plus, our family started right away. Had that not happened—had JoAnne had the opportunity to keep going to school or do something on her own outside the church, that would have helped her self-esteem and sense of security in herself.
>
> It was altogether the wrong springboard for the future—*all* those things.

JoAnne, like many brides, came into marriage expecting wonderful sharing and romance. Instead . . .

> I think I was probably in shock that whole year. I just didn't know that was how it was going to be. I didn't protest (that came later), but I couldn't believe that what I had thought would be so wonderful was reduced to my being totally alone in a strange place. I didn't have a car, so I couldn't go be with friends at the college. All I remember is fixing supper, him running in to eat—and then leaving again.

When June came, the couple retreated to JoAnne's parents' home in Owen Sound to await the birth of their child. JoAnne's father had to help with the hospital bill, while Wayne worked in a canning plant.

In the fall, they returned to Toronto to begin seminary. In time, Wayne was placed in a student pastorate, and the following year, a second son was born. Mothering consumed JoAnne's attention for the time being.

A strange lack of stamina seemed to plague her, though; in the first pastorate after seminary she found she needed an afternoon nap along with her preschoolers just to make it through the day. She caught infections easily. Says Wayne:

> I thought she was just depressed about being in the ministry. She was wiped out all the time. I kept going back and forth from guilt, for putting her in this position, to anger—"Why can't you adjust to this? You knew I was going into pastoral work."

JoAnne cast the problem in spiritual terms as well, assuming she was not dedicated enough. Only when they came to Barrie several years later did a doctor identify her low blood sugar and begin medication.

The Aagards remember Barrie, however, for another reason: here was where JoAnne finally uncorked the tension that had been building inside.

> I was just so hungry to have a relationship with Wayne. I really loved and admired him. But we didn't work as a team, because I didn't have the qualifications, plus the kids, my health, and everything.
>
> I didn't want to detract from what he was doing. But I wanted to be with him. So I went about it the wrong way. The build-up of frustration, of being "submissive" and quiet, finally reached a breaking point.
>
> When I went to a doctor about my health, I found out I had been eating all the wrong things, and diet changes would help. I didn't tell him about our [relationship] problems, but he read them anyway. He said I should throw some dishes, break some

plates, swear at my husband—and then we should go out, have a glass of wine, and talk!

When JoAnne did confront her husband at home the first time, he was mortified.

> It was a very shattering thing for me. She said I really didn't need her; she was just there to be used, take care of the house, and all I was ever concerned about was the ministry. It just floored me.
>
> I went in the living room, fell down on my knees, and began to weep. I hadn't realized I was such a rotten husband.

Wayne apologized, resolved to mend his ways, and a week later suggested they go out to dinner. JoAnne read that invitation, however, as something she had manipulated—which took all the romance out of it. What she craved was an overture from him without being prompted.

Wayne's response: "JoAnne, I *want* to do these things. I want to be with you. You have to tell me what pleases you, so I know." This approach-avoidance pattern has continued to be a difficulty throughout the marriage.

Life would seem to level out for two or three months, and then JoAnne would unburden her feelings again: Wayne didn't really love her. There really was no place for her in his life. All he cared about was the ministry. That's why he said yes to every speaking engagement that came along.

> I felt I really bared my soul, my self, my femininity, my deep person in explaining how much I needed and wanted him. Afterward, I felt somewhat cheapened to have to do it again and again, and not receive what I wanted.

The more she talked, the more confused Wayne became. His wife's relational needs seemed insatiable. He finally went for counseling, but when the counselor asked to see JoAnne as well, that embarrassed her. Another painful argument ensued.

Wayne was taking his day off a week, playing with his young sons, driving the family to a park or one of the many lakes nearby. Both spouses remember enjoyable times in Barrie along with the bad. The problem was deeper than time together; it was rather the lack of communion, a zone where husband and wife could unwind together, be safe, and share their deepest selves.

After four years in Barrie, they made a major move: out to the western prairies to a large church in Saskatoon, where Wayne would be an associate minister. By now the boys were well into their grade school years. The upheaval was difficult for JoAnne, but on the other hand, she wondered if perhaps a new setting might bring them closer to a solution.

Wayne remembers one winter night when the mercury hovered at twenty-nine below.

> We sat talking by the fireplace for a long time, just the two of us. And at the end, she said, "Well, thank you for talking to me."
>
> I thought, *Mama mia! So this is what the lady wants! OK, now I've got a clue. Run with it.*
>
> But I'd get so involved in the work that I'd forget.

Soon Wayne opted for an even longer move, a bold venture: the pastorate of the International Church in Beirut, Lebanon, in 1975. This meant enrolling their boys, now high schoolers, in the city's American High School at the semester break in January. Wayne began his ministry among this English-speaking congregation of diplomats, educators, and business types the first Sunday of February.

Everything went well—for two and a half months. On April 13, Lebanon's civil war exploded, with rightist and leftist militia as well as the PLO all determined to annihilate each other. The crown city of the Mediterranean erupted in carnage, and within two days the Canadian embassy called to say, "Evacuate to Cyprus."

Wayne and JoAnne quickly packed three suitcases, gathered their sons, and headed for the airport. The next three months were spent waiting and worrying in Nicosia. What now? All those mission dollars, contributed by hundreds of churches large and small from British Columbia to the Maritimes—down the drain. Wasted. JoAnne openly questioned whether her husband hadn't gone into the ministry out of family pressure rather than a call from God. That led to a nasty argument about whether to return to Canada and seek a different line of work. But at age forty-two? How?

Says JoAnne:

> Something died inside me there in Cyprus. I didn't feel like trying anymore. I didn't want to be hurt or vulnerable. I lost the ability to cry.
> That's still true; I'm sorry about that. So many times I just need to cry about our marriage. I don't know if that will ever change.

On July 2, as the fighting raged on in Beirut, the Aagards boarded a plane for Rome and thence to Canada. Wayne did not quit the ministry; he took a charge in Peterborough, a medium-sized city northeast of Toronto, and tried to resume pastoral work. He encouraged JoAnne to take an outside job, hoping this would diffuse her unhappiness. In that, he was correct. She received both compliments and raises at the government office where she worked as a secretary.

The church, however, was an opposite story. Wayne found himself locked in a desperate political struggle with powerful members of the Session. The question of leaving the ministry loomed in his mind all over again. But without an alternative to consider, he plunged into his work with feverish energy, lest he lose the battle at the church and be dismissed. That meant fewer nights home than ever, and more tension with JoAnne.

> I said to myself, "How can I go on being a pastor with this unresolved?" It was a spiritual defeat for me. I was going through great internal insecurities—and I was all the security JoAnne had.
> If a business opportunity had come along just then, I would

have split! I was going day and night. So once again I heard, "Your whole life is the church. What do you need me for? If you loved me, you'd be home more."

After six years of stress, both partners were relieved to escape to the quietness of Nova Scotia. The Yarmouth church has welcomed them warmly and fallen in step with Wayne's initiatives. From the upstairs parsonage windows, you can see the Atlantic Ocean, and the bobbing of the fishing boats in the harbor has been a solace to their spirits.

In some ways, their most impassioned speeches are over now, and there is no use repeating them. They talk about their relationship in quieter tones these days. A bit of light even breaks through occasionally, like the day JoAnne said, "You know, you're essentially a nonemotional person. I don't think you even have needs."

Wayne thought about that a long time and then replied, "Actually, my emotional need is to do my best in the ministry. That's my drive. Not that I'm complete in my work; when you're away, I feel very lonely. But the center of my fulfillment is what I do at the church."

That statement clarified things for JoAnne:

> While I didn't like to hear it—because I felt it excluded me—it did help me understand his behavior all these years. His job is very total for him. I can't blame him like I used to.
>
> A lot of our life together has been so good in so many ways that I should not drag up the problems, I guess. I am finding more ways to be fulfilled in ministry now. Our kids are doing well; it's a good time.
>
> We've gone to seminars and read the Christian books on marriage. But I feel as leaders there's a lot we preach that we're not putting into practice.

On Monday mornings—Wayne's day off—they drive up the shore to a favorite restaurant for breakfast together. It is a commitment he has made in his calendar to nurture the marriage. JoAnne, however, sees it differently:

The first thing he does is ask for the Halifax newspaper! We're both news junkies. So we each take a section and read—it's almost comical.

We're happy and enjoying the morning, but unless we force ourselves to talk deeply, it doesn't happen. Otherwise, we just talk about the news, go run some errands, and return home.

That's our time together—but it really accomplishes nothing to build each other up or discover ways to share insights.

Wayne, on the other hand, carries his own memories of being rebuffed. Like the proverbial ships passing in the night, their overtures to each other somehow keep missing the mark.

I get up in the morning before she does, and I'll grind the coffee, make it, and bring her a cup in bed. Before flowers got so expensive, I used to bring her roses from time to time. But the things I do that I think are romantic don't seem to get a sense of appreciation or response in warmth. So then I say to myself, *Why am I doing this?*

We've had our times of sexual coldness along the way. I've tried to be affectionate and warm without any advances—just rubbing her back, for example. My concern has been her enjoyment. But when she doesn't respond, I end up thinking, *What does it take?* I get resentful at being rejected.

A couple of years ago, in one of the tense times, I said, "Do you just want to be brother and sister? Is that the relationship you want? If so, let me know, because although I'm assertive, I'm not an army general."

She didn't answer. To talk about our sexual relationship is almost impossible. She was raised very conservatively, and although she has moved somewhat—sex is no longer dirty to her—there's still some reserve there.

JoAnne describes their physical relationship as "not growing—very ho-hum." She tells about buying a Christian book on sexual enrichment and finding it helpful. She shared it with Wayne, but he never got around to finishing it, she says. "Maybe I approached him wrong or something."

One time Wayne and I were out walking together, and I said, "Let's think of our marriage as a cruise. You be the captain, and I'll be the cruise director. I'll think up the interesting things to do!"

He said, "That would be fine."

But then there was a little ruffle of some kind. I planned something creative to do one evening, and I got the impression he wasn't so hot on the idea. We sank back into our routine.

An irritant over the years has been Wayne's love of tennis. JoAnne confesses she has "not been a nice wife" about the amount of time he has spent on the court. They say they want to begin playing together now, although JoAnne's skill level will be no challenge for her husband, and that may cause problems.

They cling to the memories of vacation trips they enjoyed together, the times when deep communication happened almost by accident. Their sons are now grown, the older one training for the ministry himself. The younger one, however, appears to have left the faith and resents what pastoring has done to his parents.

With the passing years, Wayne has come to understand himself better:

I suppose I carry the curse of perfectionism. I'm never satisfied in the ministry; I always think I could be doing better. That irritates JoAnne.

But I'm not an extemporaneous speaker who can stand up and shoot from the hip. Preaching, for me, takes *time.* If a lot of counseling comes along too, then I end up taking my reading home. And that's not good.

The process of being interviewed caused JoAnne at one point to say that in spite of everything, she still carries hope for the relationship. Her husband later expressed relief about that comment.

I was afraid she had given up, and that made me angry. I too have hope that I'll catch on and make the changes she feels I should. In this church, we have the best chance yet to get our act together.

But JoAnne also carries a darker reading of the situation:

> We know enough to do better, and have chosen not to. We're at the point now where we know what each other's going to say, so why go through it again?
>
> It would take a great deal to make me cry now. I feel the tightness in my chest; the tears are there, and I want to cry. But I steel myself and my emotions.
>
> I know Wayne loves me, and I love him. I admire and respect him, too. I just wish he needed me and would show that, without my having to beg. I am so tired of throwing myself at his feet.

And what if nothing changes? What if the deep desire for self-revelation and intimacy goes unmet?

> I'll just go on. I may not be victorious . . . but I'm a survivor.

Her husband would say the same. The two of them have breathed the word *divorce* only a few times in the heat of confrontation, and backed away from it immediately. They are too old for that . . . they hope. In the absence of progress, they will go on enduring.

REFLECTIONS
by David Seamands

The same kind of confrontation occurs in this marriage as with the Pacynskis, but the result is not so positive. After talking to a doctor who tells JoAnne to blow a fuse, she does. Wayne is shattered. But she has a desire that is found in a lot of North American women (because of television, I think): "I want my husband to do romantic things, but he mustn't plan or schedule them. They have to be spontaneous, or I can't accept them. They're not genuine if they're premeditated."

Well, Wayne Aagard is the kind of guy who isn't going to do *anything* that's not scheduled.

This is a built-in hazard of maleness and femaleness, and I see it in a lot of ministry couples. We're brainwashed—even Christians—into thinking that love, to be real, must be spontaneous. The pastor's wife especially must deal with this myth, because the nature of a pastor's work is that in order to give his wife attention and time, he will need to schedule it. If she's going to say, "That isn't real; you had me down as just another appointment, and it didn't come spontaneously out of a great overflowing Niagara Falls of love," it will kill initiative right away. The nature of the vocation is such that spontaneous moments are few and far between. (The same is true for doctors and other people-helping professionals.)

My wife used to say, "Maybe I'll go write my name in your appointment book." But we soon got beyond that as she realized the nature of the ministry, and as I scheduled prime time for just us. We put it in the church bulletin and educated the congregation to know that Monday was our "Date Day." Soon she was saying, "I can put up with almost anything for six days, because I know I've got David all day Monday."

Other aspects of the Aagard marriage are worth noting:

This pastoral family has moved a lot, and when you do that, you're constantly trying to win over new congregations. You can't afford to turn down invitations. You say, *I've got to please them*, especially in congregationally governed churches, where they can vote you out if they don't like you.

That puts a heavy burden on couples. A pastor feels he *must* please the people in order to be secure enough even to start serving the Lord.

The Aagards had their confrontation in Barrie, but JoAnne's unrealistic expectation of spontaneity booby-trapped progress. Wayne was rebuffed, and *he* then became the wounded one. He had tried to be vulnerable, but his wife had made things almost impossible, he felt, and things began to deteriorate from there.

JoAnne's stated needs are not practical in light of her husband's vocation. That vocation, of course, has never been her favorite.

She gets no reward out of his work, she says. She's not fulfilled by co-ministering with him.

I must point out that those entering the ministry these days must be much more careful about whom they marry than in the past. They cannot go on assumptions. A woman cannot say, "Well, I love him, and whatever job he wants to do in life is up to him; it doesn't concern me." That doesn't work; there *has* to be a deeper commitment if the "job" is the ministry (or medicine or law or politics). Unless the spouse finds fulfillment in this work, things will end in disaster.

Actually, there is enough suffering in the Aagard marriage to force them to solutions, but so far that has not happened. The tension has understandably affected their sexual relationship. Say what you will: A good love life sweetens a lot of bitter things. If this couple could have built intimacy from the beginning, the whole marriage might have taken a different course. Sexual problems lurk in the shadows of so many troubled couples I've counseled.

It's significant that neither one will really surrender to the other and admit needs. JoAnne gives Wayne a book on sex, and he doesn't have time for it; he ignores it. This is *indirect* communication. He attempts to do romantic things, but by this time, she is suspicious of all his motives. Every attempt on both sides is defeated by unrealistic expectations. They both have to have it their way or not at all. They forget that sex is the ultimate form of surrender—it's described that way in Scripture.

If a pastoral couple hits sexual problems early in marriage, they ought to seek help. Sexual therapy can be very important, because a good sex life is a bridge over many valleys. God intended it that way. Sex is one way he coaxed us into marriage in the first place, and it's a way he holds a lot of things together.

If a couple has a good sex life, I find they downplay it: "Oh, it's no big deal." But if they *don't* have a good sex life, it clouds every part of their horizon. They think about it a lot; it gets mixed in with every other problem.

The sadness of the Aagards is shown in that both are trying desperately to hang on to hope. They're not quite to the stage of the Emmaus disciples, who used the pluperfect tense, "We *had* hoped. . . ." But they are not far away. They seem unwilling to pay the price to achieve their dreams. And that is one of the saddest things in life: People have dreams, realize the cost, and say it's not worth the risk and pain.

I don't think this marriage is in danger of splitting. Wayne and JoAnne are committed to each other, but they've settled into sort of a ceasefire: "Maybe this is the best we can do, and we'll make the best of it." They're both quoting, "God's grace is sufficient. . . ."

In fact, they *can* do better, even at this late stage. Studies of marital satisfaction show that the highest scores occur during the middle years, as kids leave home. That's where this couple is.

I would hope Wayne might make this offer to his wife: "We need help, and we both still have a little hope. But we're kidding ourselves trying to work it out alone. So you choose the counselor, and I'll foot the bill. I'm willing to pay the price to have our hopes realized. The best years of our life can still be in the future."

SEVENTEEN

The Denzers:
JUST A HEADACHE

By the time Clair and Helen Denzer moved from their first church in an ethnic neighborhood of Cincinnati to the county seat town of El Dorado, Kansas, their son and daughter were growing up. The salary in this church was enough to provide even an annual vacation trip back east.

It was August 29, and a soft drizzle was falling as Clair drove across southern Indiana on the way home after ten days with relatives. A curve turned out to be tighter than he had estimated, and traction was lost; the car went into a skid, broke through a guardrail, and went over an embankment. Tall weeds and small saplings along the ditch slowed their momentum, and he managed to get the car stopped without overturning.

A quick check revealed no apparent injuries other than bruises. The old car, however, had been banged up considerably, to the point it was undrivable. The family spent the rest of that day in a motel in Seymour while Clair shopped for another car.

We got home two days later and seemed to be all right—but what we did not realize was that Helen had gotten a very severe whiplash. The initial stiffness in her neck went away, and she seemed fine for a while. But somewhere around Christmastime, the headaches began.

At first Helen dismissed them as tension headaches created by the holiday bustle. They continued throughout the winter, however, sometimes even preventing her from sleep.

> I got to the place where I couldn't concentrate. I was losing weight. And I couldn't stand people—which is pretty bad if you're a pastor's wife!
>
> We couldn't have visitors in our home, even our very best friends. A pastor couple from Salina drove down one time, and I just fell apart. I couldn't handle it.
>
> At one point I think I was out of church for three months. Even talking on the phone was too much.
>
> I could handle the kids. Anything inside the house was all right. But the outside world just unnerved me.

Clair, a man from strong, self-reliant roots, did the best he could to juggle a church of 140 and the needs at home. But he couldn't resist an occasional comment that urged his wife to snap out of it. When he would happen to mention a church detail—for example, that Mrs. Smith was in the hospital for an appendectomy—Helen might break out in tears. Then he would find himself saying, "Come on, what's the matter? Get hold of yourself."

Helen knew it was futile to try to explain how she was feeling, and she had no words for it anyway. In fact, she was tormented some nights with the thought that she, at the age of thirty, was having a nervous breakdown. She still did not connect the occasional pain in her neck with the other disabilities.

> The Enemy really used that to tell me, *Well, you're going to die. You're not going to live very long. You're going out of your mind. You'll soon be finished; you're no use to your husband,* and on and on.
>
> One time I remember Clair got disgusted with something I said

and responded, "Oh, come on now—don't be crazy." I thought to myself, *You don't know how right you are! I AM going crazy.*

In the midst of this, an urgent phone call came from a young couple back in Cincinnati whose wedding Clair had performed. The wife had been under severe and mysterious stress and disorientation. Would their beloved Pastor Denzer be willing to make an expenses-paid trip back to talk to her and pray with her?

Clair thought it odd, but the longer they begged, the more he sensed his coming might be a symbol of hope to the couple. He agreed to go.

Helen remembers a certain Sunday dinner just before Clair was to leave for the Wichita airport. *There he is, going to Cincinnati to pray for someone with a nervous breakdown,* she thought as she served the dessert, *and he doesn't know his own wife is having one!* But she remained locked in her quietness.

On the way home, Clair began to think deeply about his wife's condition. Maybe she really was in some kind of trouble. He arranged for her to see a chiropractor, who soon identified the problem in her neck. He began treatments and also gave Helen permission to come without an appointment whenever she felt the need. "If you just need to get away, you can relax in one of the rooms here as long as you want," he said.

That treated the physical causes and answered some of the questions harassing Helen's mind. But by this time, her depression and fears were planted firmly enough that they had taken on life of their own. She was still traumatized by the thought of mixing in a crowd of church people or playing the piano for a service once again. "I have no one I can counsel with!" she once lamented to Clair. "I don't have a pastor; there's no one I can talk to."

Gradually her husband began tempering his impatience and listening more to her expressions of panic. He began praying for her, out loud, in her presence. He also began to show more understanding.

People in the church were compassionate and loving, often sending in food. Those who had undergone nervous problems of their own were especially sympathetic. One man told her, "When I was having my hard time, my doctor used to say, 'It's all in your head.' And I'd say, 'I know that; what I want you to tell me is how to get it out!' "

A breakthrough did not come, however, until Helen's mother arrived from Cleveland. She ended up staying six weeks, taking over in the kitchen and the laundry room and also giving major doses of Scripture and prayer. Helen vividly remembers:

> By that time I was at a point where I couldn't cry—the tears were all gone. I couldn't emote, I couldn't laugh. I could talk about the normal routine, but I didn't smile very much. I couldn't pray, either.
>
> One of the first things—because I was full of so many fears—was every morning after breakfast, she would have me sit while she prayed over me and read the Bible. "You just sit and receive while I pray and read," she'd say. "I know you can do that much."
>
> That went on for several weeks, every day. It was during those sessions that healing began to come in.

Sometime in the third week, Helen found herself able to pray again. As she did, the tears resumed their flow. The next Sunday morning she tried going to church and found it manageable.

Sitting in the sanctuary that day, she remembered an event that had happened almost a year before, when her trial was just beginning. She had been playing a postlude for a service like this one. All at once Isaiah 41:10 had been uniquely quickened to her—"Fear thou not; for I am with thee: be not dismayed; for I am thy God: I will strengthen thee; yea, I will help thee; yea, I will uphold thee with the right hand of my righteousness." The word *uphold* had burned in her mind, as if to say, *You can't go under; God is upholding you.*

It had really been a very dark year. But the Lord had held me from collapsing, and he had also brought my mother out to minister to me at just the right time.

As his wife began to improve, Clair finally saw a reason for the ordeal.

Suddenly the *real* purpose came to me: it was for *me*. I was always very short with people who complained about being nervous. I had a hard time being compassionate.

I learned there was a lot more than just "taking hold of yourself" like I'd been telling people to do. These nerve problems were very, very real.

Helen's Sunday morning attendance gradually expanded to Sunday evenings as well, and then to a full schedule. The Denzers decided to celebrate with a shopping trip.

My husband took me to an expensive dress shop—it was really a treat. We picked out this pink dress together. I remember feeling so good coming out of that store. It was like a new beginning for me.

I felt great, and I looked good in the dress . . . and about a month later, I became pregnant and had to put it in the closet!

Helen wore that dress later on, however, and kept wearing it as long as the style would allow—a symbol of her recovery. The baby boy born that November became "my tonic child," she says, because of the joy and strength he seemed to stimulate within her.

The dark year was twenty-five years ago now, but Helen Denzer still tells the story occasionally when she speaks to women's groups. They listen to this voice of experience and find the encouragement to press on for wholeness.

REFLECTIONS
by David Seamands

Ministers, it seems, do enjoy better health than the average. This is probably because they are very fulfilled in their work, which helps health. But it also can leave them insensitive to the physical weaknesses of their wives.

Because women express illness more openly and emotionally, husbands often oversimplify and overspiritualize. Many a minister with a sick wife almost views her as part of his spiritual reputation. It's like having a wayward teenage son or daughter. Ministers can be very cruel about this: "I'm bearing this cross; my poor wife isn't spiritual; she's always ill, always depressed."

A lot of ministers' wives I counsel show considerable resentment about this: "He doesn't understand. He has time for everyone else's illness but mine. He's making hospital calls every week of the year, but when I get sick, it's a different story."

I admit that early in my own marriage, I too was guilty of inferring that if my wife were spiritually OK, she wouldn't be sick. I've had to ask forgiveness for that.

Helen Denzer enjoyed a lot of blessings, however, in her case: a caring congregation, a terrific mother who understood and was helpful, and the discovery of purpose and meaning in it all. Because she could believe God was using this, she would emerge a stronger minister's wife, understanding people better.

It's *meaningless* suffering that destroys us. If we can see a purpose, we can stand just about anything. Victor Frankl discovered in the concentration camps that the human spirit can take any *what* if it can discover a *why*. Holocaust survivors were those who saw some kind of meaning in it.

The other lesson in the Denzer experience is that recovery from breakdown takes a *lot* of time. There's no quickie cure. Many ministers don't understand that. This is especially true of emotional or nervous breakdown—which is what this became because it was oversimplified in the beginning. An emotional breakdown is almost like all the computers in the Pentagon going down at once. How do you hold the outlying troops in control? You can't, until the center is rebuilt slowly but surely.

Or it's like falling over a cliff. The climb back to the top takes a lot longer than the fall. You have to be patient with yourself. This wonderful mother was so patient with Helen; she was the key to the recovery. She stopped her daughter from condemning herself for taking so long to get well.

If you're sick, that's bad enough; but if you have guilt on top of it, that's doubly bad. Instead of sixteen tons, you're carrying thirty-two. We're all made for sixteen, but nobody's made for thirty-two.

(Isn't it interesting that the recovery in this case included a pregnancy? Between the lines there, I think I see a breakthrough of affection. She calls her new son "my tonic child"—what a beautiful phrase.)

EIGHTEEN

The DeJongs:
PIERCING THE VEIL

Terese DeJong has spent ten years of her life—a full decade—putting her husband through the last half of a B.A., two master's degrees, and a doctorate. She is a crack legal secretary who can keep code numbers and deposition details in her head without missing a *whereas* at eighty-five words per minute. Neither she nor her husband intended to be in the pastorate; Paul had had enough of that growing up as a minister's son. He rather wanted a Ph.D., and Terese wanted to see him get it.

Toward that end, they endured the usual stresses of seminary, he soaring into the academic stratosphere (but also working as a part-time youth pastor) while she earned most of the income—and had a baby. They passed each other in the apartment complex hallway more than once. Communication time was spasmodic. Terese remembers:

> He'd come home and try some of his far-out theological ideas on me—and I had this little fundamentalist faith. I couldn't even understand him half the time. We went to church together, of course, but I really wasn't growing spiritually.

Paul frankly accuses seminary in those days of being a head trip that drove people apart rather than pulling them together.

> It wasn't that I didn't respect Terese for her knowledge. But I had suddenly become the fount of all truth. It was the worst possible strain on a marriage.
>
> I had hoped to go on to graduate study in England, but during my last year she became pregnant again, and we couldn't afford it. That was a good thing; any more study probably *would* have killed us.

So for the time being, the DeJongs came to First Reformed Church of Smyrna, Delaware. Their little girl was born in May, Paul received his M.Div. in June, and they moved the first of July to a town of four thousand. The first year was difficult for the two of them, until a crisis forced Paul to stop bullying her intellectually and led Terese to find meaning in her work as a wife and mother, not just in the workplace.

Later on, they returned to the campus to finish Paul's education, after which they returned to pastoring. The congregation they serve today in Grand Rapids, Michigan, is solid, appreciative, and in the midst of a building program. Paul is not what would be termed a workaholic pastor; he gives the church full measure but takes his fathering responsibilities seriously as well. The years of schooling are now being put to good use in preaching and teaching. "He has a great ability to take hard things and make them simple," says his wife with admiration. "I don't think people fully notice the benefits of all his graduate work."

The academic sculpting of Paul DeJong, however, with its many hours of deep concentration, has created a man who does not quickly shift gears. His body can move from book-lined office to family rec room faster than his mind.

> Some days I come home, and I just can't sit down; I keep walking around. I don't want to do that, but I do. I'm not mad at

anybody—I just can't stop the energy. I don't have a solution for that yet.

The ministry is doubly preoccupying, I think. If I were a businessman, I'd probably be the same way. But on top of that, this is eternal stuff.

Also, the more finely trained your mind is, the more you use it to try to solve everything. You don't just let things go. You keep mulling them over.

He happens, of course, to be married to an action-oriented woman, the legal secretary who thrives on pressure and is always thinking of what comes next. She freely admits:

I hate procrastination in any form, in anybody. I like everything all sewed up. Part of the struggle Paul has with me is that I'm such a controlling person. I try to sew up *his* loose ends—things in his ministry where he could be more sensitive, for example—and he doesn't respond well to my saying so.

So preoccupation is one way he keeps me at bay. I don't have the power to bring him out of it. I'll be talking away about something, and suddenly I'll realize he doesn't hear. So I'll say, "I just love having conversations with myself out loud."

And he'll look up and say, "What?"

He doesn't mean to ignore me. He cares deeply about me and loves me. He's just got something on his mind.

The one trick Terese has discovered is to get Paul out of town. Once he physically leaves Grand Rapids, he relaxes and in some ways reverts to the funmaker he was in seminary. She relishes the time they headed north one March and got stranded by a snowstorm in a Petoskey, Michigan, motel. They talked and laughed together like old times.

But on another winter trip, things backfired. They were flying to Florida, where Paul was to speak at a conference. When the plane made a stopover at Tampa, he got out to breathe the warm gulf air. Paul is a confirmed snow hater, and the blessings of a warm climate mesmerized him there outside the terminal. No wonder people up north came here to escape.

He returned to his seat on the airplane and said to Terese, "You know, the thought hit me that I could get off here and get lost, and never be found again." That was all.

She said nothing but sat reviewing the recent weeks for clues to explain his comment. Her guesswork soon got out of hand.

> What a thing to tell me! Was he really thinking about leaving me or what?
>
> We stayed at this beautiful condominium that week right by the ocean, and I didn't have his attention the whole time. True, he had to speak, plus some friends were staying there with us, but still. . . .
>
> A couple of weeks later, he went with a tour group to Israel. While he was gone, I woke up in the middle of one night thinking about that remark in Tampa. What if he never came back?! What would I do? I just panicked. So often these days you hear or read about someone walking out, and the partner being "so surprised." I couldn't think of anything wrong between us, but what if there was?
>
> See, that's where his preoccupation gets scary. I don't always know what he's thinking.

The truth is, while Terese lay terrified in Michigan, Paul was feeling downright amorous in Tel Aviv. He went for a walk one evening by himself, and the thought occurred to him that his marriage was one of God's special acts of grace in his life. To have a wife who loved him and never stopped, no matter how he behaved, was indeed an undeserved favor from above. Here was theology in the specific. He would have to tell her this when he got home.

That led to a special conversation upon his return. A great sigh of relief swept over Terese. Her fears had been groundless.

Will there be more such unveilings in the future? Both partners would like that, if they can keep finding the key. The practicalities, though, are sometimes troublesome.

> TERESE: Anything that goes wrong with me, I can tell Paul. But I sense he can't do it back. And over the years, that's been his way

of handling me—it's a power thing. I warble about everything going through my mind, so that by now, he's got all this "stuff" on me. But I don't get it back.

PAUL: Part of it is just my conviction not to tell you stuff that goes on here [at the church: board meetings, etc.]. You don't need that junk in your life.

TERESE: But you also leave out what's going on inside you.

PAUL: Yeah, I do. When things happen, I like to think about them a long time before I say them.

TERESE: Which gives you the air of being preoccupied.

PAUL: Part of that is being male. Part of it's the ministry. And part of it's just me.
I made a New Year's resolution last week: two times this year we're going off on a weekend together, and ten times this year we're going out on a date.

During a separate interview later on, Terese expressed amazement at this vow. "That's new for Paul," she claimed. "If he keeps going that way, everything's going to be cool!"

Both spouses say they are making progress in this area, gradually clearing a two-way channel of deep communication. That they are still working on it, after twenty years of marriage, is a mark of its importance. It is also a testimony to their determination not to be isolated under the same roof.

REFLECTIONS
by David Seamands

This case illustrates another hazard of the ministry. The very characteristic that makes Paul DeJong a good minister—his ability to concentrate intensely upon a segment of something—creates problems in his marriage. It has done the same in mine.

Concentration is a great gift, especially for pastors. They can focus on what they're doing at the time and exclude a lot of distractions.

Women are somewhat more holistic in their thinking. New neurological studies of the differences between male and female brains (most of them by feminists, interestingly) are bringing this out. When a little girl walks into a strange room, she is more frightened because she sees and senses everything at once; it all comes at her. The boy sees just one thing; he concentrates on that and fails to notice the rest.

When Paul DeJong says he comes home from the church office and can't stop walking around, he reveals this aspect of his male brain. It makes him a good minister but a poor husband.

Terese's insecurity in the Tampa airport incident seems unusual at first, since she is a controller, a doer, a person with no loose ends. Why should she fear? But beneath that, she is also uncertain over the years about where her husband is coming from; he's in this ethereal world, she feels. She also feels mismatched against his great education, and she downgrades her own gifts by comparison.

She may have also been thinking, *You know, he could get off here and get so fascinated with Tampa he'd forget he's married and has a family; he could get so compartmentalized he'd just leave us hanging.* If so, no wonder she was insecure.

I am fortunate to have a wife who confronts me with preoccupation. She just will not let me get by. I would really have self-destructed otherwise. She keeps pushing: "Hey, I know you're there; *talk* to me. Put those papers down. You're hearing me, but you're thinking about your next lecture or something. *Look at me* when we talk. Look me in the eye."

I know I need to do this. I even tell my classes, "You can't do two things at once if listening's one of them." But I don't always live that.

This couple has discovered that if they schedule a getaway, they can break the barrier. (The scheduling aspect is no problem to Terese; she recognizes it's that or nothing.) Paul has even resolved to schedule more opportunities in the future. The ten dates a year are a bare minimum, in my view, almost a sop. He should schedule even more prime time.

But Terese is obviously helping him with this problem. She will always have to live with his personality type, of course. These two people perceive the world differently; that's all there is to it. Nevertheless, this marriage has a lot of promise.

NINETEEN

The Scullys:
MIND GAMES

The congregational storm that struck the Arcola Christian Church four months after Nick Scully's arrival centered on him, but it was not of his making. He and Diane thought they had been simply following the board's direction, shopping for a home on the basis that the church would loan them a down payment.

When the matter came to a business meeting for approval, however, objections popped up immediately. Nick soon realized the members had not been informed of the board's promise. "What if you leave in a couple of years?" one man demanded. "Why should the church help you buy a home for yourself?"

Nick and Diane excused themselves from the meeting, promising to adjust to whatever the members voted. The motion was defeated that night, and the couple ended up arranging other housing.

Nick's relaxed manner in the pulpit was another bone of contention for some in the pews. True to their Missouri temperament, a fair number took a "Show me" attitude toward this couple from Pennsylvania. People commented about their "accent."

Attendance most Sundays held at around seventy, the level it had been before the Scullys came. But after a couple of years, one family decided to leave, then another. A church in the next town seemed more to their liking. When the third family pulled out, a definite pinch was felt in the church's finances.

Nick fell into a dark mood. His failures in an earlier church now haunted him. Diane was surely disappointed, he assumed, that he couldn't seem to make this church grow. He was disappointed in himself. What was wrong with his ministry?

> It was along about then that I began to wonder, just once in a while, if maybe things would be different if Diane were not my wife. *If she were dead, what would happen if I were married to someone else?*
>
> I certainly wasn't hoping for such a thing; it was just *Would things be easier?* I felt she was blaming me that the church hadn't blossomed here. She hadn't actually attacked me. But I would receive her comments and suggestions as that.

A young widow in the church, three years younger than Nick, came often for counseling. She had one child. Life without a husband was grinding her down, and she did not know how to handle the way she felt toward a certain man at work. What should she do?

Nick responded with the appropriate words of counsel and prayer. She was indeed an attractive woman, he thought, with a great capacity to love. The void in her life longed to be filled. She warmly appreciated Nick's gentleness with her week by week.

Before long, Nick began to realize that the woman's desire was no longer toward the fellow employee but rather her pastor. She always dressed her nicest when she came to his office, and her unspoken manner conveyed her deep regard.

Meanwhile, Nick ruminated at times about his own somewhat constrained physical relationship with Diane. Throughout their eight years of marriage so far, fulfillment had been less than he had expected. The two of them did not always see alike regarding frequency, and Nick sometimes thought of his wife as "cold."

Says Diane regarding the sexual side of marriage:

> I'm not a real passionate person. I can take it or leave it, to tell you the truth. And so, it's something I have to work at. Whereas for him, he's a man, it's "an important part of our marriage."
>
> Except for reproduction, I think I could do without it. . . . But that's not true, either. If he were suddenly taken from me, it would be hard to go without.
>
> He wants it at a different time than I want it, I guess. That's the main problem.

About three months after the counseling began, a special concern arose in the little congregation: the church treasurer's nephew was on trial for murder. He had never attended the church, but his relatives were worried. Through the treasurer he had sent a message several months before that he would like to talk to a minister.

Nick had driven to the prison several times. The young man had made no spiritual commitment, but he remained open. When the trial began twenty-two miles away in the county seat town of Lamar, Nick met with him each morning for prayer before court resumed.

Several members of the church accompanied their minister to sit in the gallery each day. The young widow and a friend of hers were among the most faithful. Nick recalls:

> On a couple of days, the other woman couldn't go, so the two of us drove together. By then it was obvious to me that she viewed me in a special light.
>
> My fantasies began to pick up speed, as you might imagine. It was that stretch of days that really showed me, *Hey, this is getting too hot to handle. I am putting myself in a situation that's going to lead to trouble.*
>
> In my own physical actions, I was above board. I don't think she ever realized the attraction was two-way. But in my mind, I knew I was wrong.

By the time the trial was over (the man was acquitted), Nick knew what he must do. The previous fall he had heard a popular seminar leader in Kansas City talk about male-female relationships and warn against raising expectations that cannot legitimately be fulfilled. Was he guilty of that, even though there had been no actual intimacy? Apparently so.

One night the next week, he and Diane sat talking in their living room. The children were asleep. After a while Diane—usually the one to introduce serious topics—said, "Are there any problems?"

Her husband looked away. "Yeah."

"What do you mean?"

"Well, up until recently I was having a hard time controlling my thought life. I didn't want to say anything until I could promise you it was over."

"Is there another woman?"

"No, not really." Nick took a long pause. "I've just been struggling with whether another gal in the church would understand me more." He then went on to breathe the name.

Diane swallowed but kept her composure.

> I had thought *something* must be happening to him. But I hadn't thought about *that*.
>
> I said, "Well, you'll either have to drop that, or we'll have to do something for a while until you can get straightened out. Maybe I could go and stay with my folks for a while or . . ." I can't remember the exact words, but I let him know I couldn't put up with him fantasizing about one woman and having me, too.
>
> In a way, though, I did feel bad for him, because maybe I wasn't being everything to him I should be. That doesn't give any excuse, of course. The pressures and problems [in the church] bother me and make me more nervous than they do him, I guess.

Nick talks about the relief he felt:

> That open confession did a lot to seal off the problem and remove it from my heart.
>
> It would be easy for me to say I've never stooped so low as to

have a physical relationship with another woman. But I have to remember what Jesus said about lust inside your head. That's what the Lord was really showing me: There was no way to continue a healthy relationship [with Diane] while my mind was taken up with fantasy.

Shortly after that, Nick mentioned from the pulpit that he was changing his ground rules for personal ministry. He had decided to counsel women only in the presence of their husbands, or a friend, or Diane. He said he felt this was a precaution he should have practiced from the beginning of his ministry. Afterward, several women in the congregation expressed their agreement with his new policy.

The young widow came to see the Scullys a few weeks later. She confessed the only reason she had gone to the courtroom was to be with Nick. She apologized to Diane for the damage she had caused.

Relationships with this woman have maintained a certain distance since then, but she has remained in the church, and no further incidents have occurred.

Nick's courage to confess to his wife not only cemented his decision but also established an important pattern for the future. Two years later, Diane found herself edging toward a similar problem with sexual fantasy. She conquered it by following her husband's example:

> Things in our marriage were getting sort of humdrum, and I felt like I needed something more exciting. I began inventing someone who would give me that. No one man in particular, nobody I knew—just an imaginary person.
>
> I didn't realize it at the time, but now that I look back on it, a lot of this was coming from evening TV. Nick was gone a lot, and I'd watch all this stuff, and after a while, it looks normal. You start thinking, *Why isn't my marriage like that?*
>
> I had to tell Nick about it. I didn't want to. I felt like *I can handle this. I'll just stop, and no one needs to know.* It's very humbling to have to tell somebody you were so weak to do something so stupid.

But I realized that in order to stop, I needed to tell him. And of course, he was extremely understanding. That was when I really gained victory.

The Scullys have since taken the bold step of banning all secular television from their home. Some in their church think this is "fanatical," but Nick and Diane insist it promotes health, not only for themselves but for their children. Says she: "Since those shows are out now, I don't have to live up to anything."

Their public ministry, in the meantime, goes on steadily, and they are learning to let one another help carry the frustrations of ministry. Whether the church grows or not, they will stick with each other, not a chimera. Nick smiles convincingly as he says:

There's not a lady around who could ever take Diane's place. We've gone through so many things together that no one could replace her.

REFLECTIONS
by David Seamands

This case, and the two that follow it, show us a curious fact: sexual temptations are apparently greatest at the extremes. When a person's ministry is difficult and frustrating, sex can be a way to escape. But on the other hand, the height of success is also a danger zone.

We notice that age has nothing to do with anything in these cases.

Ministerial infidelity is indeed becoming more frequent, I am sorry to say. We ministers are products of our culture; there are no moral fences anymore. Have you watched this talk show on some TV stations called *Good Sex?* When my generation was growing up, we may have jumped the fence sometimes, but at least we knew the fence was there.

When Vance Packard wrote *The Sexual Wilderness*, he was asked to call it *The Sexual Revolution* instead. He replied that a revolution has *goals*. You may go through chaos to reach them, but you know where you're going. The modern sexual scene, he said, was not a march to new goals; it was more like a wide-open plain. I found that comment very profound, especially from a secular social psychologist.

This has certainly affected the church and its leaders.

I must admit I had trouble reading some of these narratives, because I too have struggled to keep my thought life clean and holy. All other battles pale in significance to that one. I remember talking to a saintly missionary years ago who was in his seventies. I asked him to name his greatest temptations. Quick as a flash he said, "Sex and self."

I'm really grateful for a tough, confrontive wife and the grace of God. Those are the outside forces that have rescued me at times.

Every case of unfaithfulness starts, of course, in rationalizing that fantasy is allowable. Nick Scully's first fantasy is *What if Diane would die?* (I used to preach a sermon in which I would rather casually ask the men in the audience, "Stop a minute and think about what if your wife should die. Do you already have somebody picked out?" The place always got stone-silent! I just let the subject drop at that point; the fallout spoke for itself.)

The sex life in the Scully marriage is less than satisfactory. So there are frustrations in the bedroom as well as in the church—a *deadly* combination. Add to that an aggressive young widow, and trouble is ensured.

There are women who, because of their psychological past, find a kind of satisfaction in knocking ministers, lawyers, and others in high positions off their pedestals. I don't know that this widow had this in mind, but I do believe ministers should be warned about it. Some women are out for them, and they may be very religious women who are unconscious of what they're doing, but . . . they will still try to bring the minister down.

Why do they do this? If you want to be Freudian, I suppose you would say these women want to get even with men, or with *somebody*.

I remember one counselee who used to come in the summertime dressed very carelessly. One day she arrived in shorts and a very brief top. So for my own protection as much as anything else,

I brought the problem right out into the open. I said, "It's obvious to me what you are out to do by the way you're dressing and sitting. . . . Well, you are succeeding. You have sexually aroused me. *Now* what are your plans?"

She was shocked. She broke down at that point and admitted this was a major problem. We had a very good talk after that, in which some truth came out about her relationship to her husband, her fantasy affairs, and so forth.

Not every woman who gets involved with a minister is this kind, certainly. But many are.

The other danger in counseling is that transference, or whatever you want to call it, is sometimes absolutely essential to the healing of the person. This fact bothers me. It's true: I must *reparent* some women. I am a father to them.

But they sometimes fall in love and want more than a father. Scores of times I've had to bring this out into the open.

Nick Scully did an extremely wise thing when he shared with his wife. In my own marriage, I have always been very open about these things, making them into a humorous game. I'll say, "You know, that gal really gets to me somehow. I could go for her," and my wife will say, "Well, I find so-and-so very attractive." We kid each other, but in so doing we pour Lysol on the matter and keep it antiseptic.

And Diane Scully was wise with her *tough love*. She took a firm line from the start—there was no sloppy agape. She said OK, you can't have your cake and eat it too. It's me or her.

That doesn't sound very Christian—but it is.

Contrast this with the "Christian wife who's so loving." Her great mistake is apathy. I remember one woman who was so kind, so willing to forgive her non-Christian husband for an affair. Later on, he came to see me and said, "You know, I know she's trying to be nice—but I was hurt. I don't know whether she really loves me or not. I wish she'd gotten madder than hell. Then I'd know she really cares."

The minister must know that 100 percent of his emotional fulfillment and enjoyment must come from his wife—nobody else. You see, in the ministry there *is* emotional fulfillment from other women. The majority of the members and even a higher percentage of the attendees are women. In every congregation, some of them flatter, they gush—and if you're not careful, you can believe their tripe after a while. That's dangerous.

In the face of any indiscretion, anger and resentment are always better than accommodation. A holy jealousy is a sign of a true love. Awhile ago the television program *20/20* had a half-hour segment on "the problem of jealousy," which was portrayed as a terrible vice. We should train husbands and wives not to be jealous.

I got so mad I preached that Sunday on "The Lord thy God is a *jealous* God." I cited a lot of Old Testament texts about God's jealousy for his bride Israel and said, "Look—jealousy is part of the character of God. We are made in his image. If we think we can dispose of that characteristic, God have mercy on us."

I did point out that there is an insane jealousy, of course—the kind that sends some people reaching for a shotgun when trouble arises. That's not what I'm advocating. The tough line that guards a marriage, however, is *not wrong.* I've dealt with a lot of affair situations over the years, and if a minister starts down this path, it's awfully hard for him to stop unless his wife throws crockery and makes a royal scene. Otherwise, he will destroy himself.

When Nick Scully, in telling his wife about his fantasies, said he had waited until he could promise her it was over, I think he was deceiving himself. I don't think it was as "over" at that instant as he wanted to believe. But he had enough moral integrity to know that sharing it with Diane *would* help him cross the line. That's why he did it. It's like what counselees have sometimes told me: "Just by making an appointment with you, I solved my problem."

Later on, of course, Diane defeated *her* temptations the same way, and that's the marvelous part of this story. She shared her fantasies with Nick.

Here is someone who is allegedly "cold" in her sexual life, and yet she reaches a season where that part of life spins out of control. Blessed is the wife whose husband has shared in this way, so that when *her* time of temptation comes, she shares it with him.

Their decision against all secular television reminds me of Ed Wheat's advice in his book *Intended for Pleasure* that newlywed couples ought to throw out the TV for the first year. Their love life will develop much better.

TWENTY

The Ewings:
A TRAGEDY OF ERRORS

What happened to Gary and Pamela Ewing within the first year of pastoring is lamentable enough, apart from the fact it could easily have been prevented more than once. Their story is a patent example of why the apostle Paul, in two different chapters of 1 Timothy, warned against granting ministry responsibility too soon. "Lay hands suddenly on no man," he wrote (5:22), especially "not a novice, lest being lifted up with pride he fall into the condemnation of the devil" (3:6).

Growing up in the small Idaho town of Wendell, Gary and Pam were high school sweethearts who got married at the ages of eighteen and sixteen because a baby was on the way. The censure they felt from Pam's parents and the townspeople—especially church members—sealed off any spiritual inclinations, which were minimal to start with. Gary took a few night classes at a vo-tech school in nearby Twin Falls but soon found he was good at selling, and for the next six years money was his god. The young couple scrambled, acquired, moved often, had two more children, and lived like normal American pagans. Gary's natural leadership abilities and gregarious nature dominated the marriage, Pam sticking quietly to her kitchen and her babies.

The family darkened the door of a church only because Gary wanted to play on its softball team, for which attendance was a requirement. The Christ they met there was willing to accept and forgive them. They became Christians. The change in their lives was genuine. Says Gary:

> I sort of lost my desire to get rich. I felt my life had been mostly a waste up to then. I didn't want to give up my lifestyle, but I wanted to be and do what God wanted me to do.
>
> My "killer instinct" as a salesman seemed to escape me, and I wasn't sure what that meant. I still had to feed my family somehow, but selling wasn't as much fun as it used to be.

After four years of active participation in the church, doing everything from driving a Sunday school bus to singing, Gary heard about a lucrative distributorship available in Las Cruces, New Mexico. He uprooted the family for the thousand-mile move, and they soon joined a church.

Gary was given an adult Sunday school class to teach, and the room quickly filled up. He peppered his pastor with doctrinal questions, eager to learn all he could. Finally one day he said, "You know, maybe I should go to Bible school."

Pastor Coffey promptly handed him a brochure and a catalog about the denominational college in Memphis. Soon afterward, Gary put the house up for sale, packed up once again, and headed east.

The first year was rugged. The family lived on its savings and what could be earned through weekend church meetings at which they sang. As summer approached, Gary began lining up an itinerary of churches and camps back in the Northwest. This former salesman at least knew how to work a prospect list.

And that was how they came to the small, pastorless congregation at Burley, Idaho. The board chairman who hosted them that evening insisted on showing Gary the parsonage after the concert was over. Gary had no intention of interrupting his schooling, and intended to be an evangelist once he finished.

But two weeks later, as their tour was nearly finished and the weariness of life on the road—a different bed every night—was taking its toll, the state presbyter called. "Are you ready to take that church in Burley?" he wanted to know. Gary thought a minute about the advantages of a regular paycheck and said yes. The matter was settled right there. By September 1, the thirty-year-old father of three with the ready smile, engaging personality, and quiet wife became a pastor, despite only one year of formal training. He would try to pick up more classes by extension, he told himself.

The first Sunday morning, Gary found himself preaching to a congregation of thirteen. Among the first thoughts that crossed his mind, he remembers, was that this church had better grow fast if he didn't want to starve. The salary agreement, modest though it was, meant nothing if the treasury was empty. Plus, the denomination required a 22 percent slice of all local receipts no matter what. Gary had his work cut out for him.

Soon new people did begin to come, including a collection of young bikers. The congregation began taking on a Heinz 57 look, but the mood was definitely up as the numbers increased. In contrast to the unusual types was a couple named Don and Rachel Fontaine. With their two little girls, they looked fit for the cover of a family magazine, and Gary breathed a silent thanksgiving for their interest and involvement. Rachel, in fact, was a minister's daughter.

By the next spring, attendance was running in the seventies, and the pastor was given a raise. That was good, because Pamela Ewing was now expecting; their fourth child would be born in June. The condition of the church immensely pleased the presbyter, who congratulated Gary and told him to keep doing whatever had brought the success thus far.

Rachel Fontaine soon began telling her pastor about the problems in her marriage and also her deep resentment of her mother. Gary took it in stride.

I was going to be one of those pastors who was above reproach and didn't have to flinch every time a woman had a problem. I could minister to people without having hangups. I'd heard all the stories about pastors getting involved with women in the church, and I figured the guy must have been looking for it.

Rachel later volunteered to paint the interior of the parsonage. It was a welcome offer, since Gary lacked the time and Pam was far along in her pregnancy. Day after day, the young housewife would stop by to work on the project.

One bright spring day, over iced tea at the kitchen table, she broke down and began to cry. She told the pastoral couple she felt like running away. Soon Pam Ewing had to leave to drive a daughter to a swimming lesson; it was then that Rachel confessed she was in love with another man—a gas station attendant in town. Gary patted her arm and said, "You have a wonderful husband and two little girls who really need you. We're just not going to let this happen." They prayed together.

That evening she stopped back at the parsonage, distraught, and insisted on seeing her pastor again. Gary went out to her van to talk, since his children were at the kitchen table eating. There she announced, "I lied to you this morning. It's not the guy at the station. You're the guy. You're driving me crazy! I just can't take it anymore."

Gary was shocked. He still remembers his response: "This can't be—I'm fifty pounds overweight!" He then said he was sure she would feel differently tomorrow. He followed that remark with the fatal error of suggesting she come to the church office in the morning to talk.

That night, Gary hardly slept. His own marriage was badly deteriorated, he told himself; Pam didn't really appreciate him, was cold to his romances, stayed in her own quiet world. The struggles of the past few years, the hand-to-mouth living, the moving, the tensions of trying to rejuvenate this church— not much had gone very well in recent times. And now *this* complication . . .

I really believed Rachel would come the next morning and tell me how sorry she was, or else she would be too ashamed to appear at all. But part of me, I must confess, hoped she would show up. As I got to the office, I remember telling God I needed help, because I felt out of control. I was suddenly very alone.

Rachel showed up that morning, a big smile on her face, dressed to dazzle. She once again recounted the stories of her husband's failures and abuses. Then suddenly she began talking about how she had always wanted to be a pastor's wife. She was so happy she had finally found Gary. It was as if Pam no longer existed. Gary recalls:

> Like a dummy, I sat there and took it all in. I remember her flashing those brown eyes at me and saying, "I think you're *terrific.*" I suddenly realized it had been a long time since I'd heard those words from anyone. I grew two feet.
>
> Rachel knew me better than I knew myself. She was always a step ahead of me.
>
> I finally pulled myself together and told her I was married and had three kids, and what she was talking about could never be. Her only choice was to go home and work things out with her husband. They needed marriage counseling, and I was not in a position to provide it.
>
> She didn't even seem to hear me. "My mother told me once when I was a girl that I could get anything in life I wanted if I wanted it bad enough," she said. "That's what I intend to do."

When she left, Gary placed an urgent phone call to Bill Coffey in New Mexico, who directed him to tell two people: his wife and the state presbyter. Gary set up a lunch with his superior for the next day. There he spilled the story.

The man told Gary first to tell his wife and second to tell Rachel to leave the church if she could not control herself. If that did not stop her, Gary should threaten to tell her husband. When Gary hinted at the struggle he was feeling inside, the presbyter said, "This kind of thing happens all the time in the ministry. You're the master of the situation. You can handle it. By the way, your church hasn't been sending in the budget portions on time. We want you to send them in on a weekly basis from now on."

Budget portions?! Gary's mind reeled. Here he was in the crisis of his life, and his leader wanted to talk about dollars for headquarters.

Back home, Gary did talk to his wife. He told her he was being chased, but he kept quiet about his own feelings. Pam showed little reaction. To this country girl, life with Gary had always seemed tumultuous. She would continue to be his follower, and whatever came in the future, she would accept.

Gary, however, was disappointed.

> I'd hoped she would have been ready to scratch this woman's eyes out. I asked if she wanted to go with me to talk to Rachel, and she said she didn't think that was necessary.
>
> I got angry. Here I had another woman throwing herself at my feet, and Pam acted like she didn't even care. Why was I staying with a woman who didn't even want me? The only reason she stayed was that she was pregnant and didn't know what else to do. I felt like a fool.

Gary called another pastor friend two hours away, who said he would come to Burley to see him. Later on, however, the man canceled for lack of time.

Meanwhile, Rachel continued stopping by the church on nearly a daily basis. He remembers praying alone at the altar more than one morning, coming to a firm resolve—"and then she'd show up, and I'd be a mess again. She always knew the right things to say."

A month went by. Finally one Thursday, Gary summoned the courage to tell her it was over. He was not going to tolerate this relationship any longer. Either Rachel had to leave the church, or he was going to resign. That, of course, brought a flood of tears.

The following Sunday was a potluck dinner at the church to celebrate the year's successes. Attendance hit an all-time high of ninety-two. While the meal was in progress, Rachel was suddenly discovered to be weeping uncontrollably in the sanctuary. A woman and then the board chairman came to Gary to suggest he see what was wrong.

Gary panicked inside to think what she might be saying to her would-be comforters. He went to her side, asked the others to leave, and then said, "What's going on?"

"I can't live without you!" she sobbed. They talked quietly for half an hour, Gary reinforcing Thursday's decision that the two of them must be only friends. The danger of exposure passed.

The next morning, Rachel was back to the church. She walked in, threw her arms around him, planted a kiss, and announced she had no intention of quitting.

From here on, the events of Gary Ewing's life proceed almost like a soap opera, only they actually happened. Pam gave birth that Saturday to another daughter. Within days, Rachel had thrown her husband out of the house and begun divorce proceedings. Actual adultery began soon afterward and continued steadily for the next two months. Gary remembers the first time:

> It was a Monday—the toughest day of a pastor's week, I guess. I was upset with Pam over something.
>
> I think I had the attitude *This is going to happen anyway; I might as well get it over with.* Rachel stopped by, and we ended up in the church nursery. It wasn't something planned for that day; it just happened.
>
> Afterward, I was amazed that I felt no guilt. That really bothered me. I thought I must really be rotten to feel no remorse for what had happened.

Gary left town at one point for a four-day trip to Alberta, to try to clear his head. When he returned, he and Pam had a major argument, although she did not know how far the affair had gone. Throughout the summer, he continued to meet

Rachel at Twin Falls motels or out in the country; she had a commodious van.

I had never been around anyone with whom I felt so comfortable. I guess I unloaded my whole life to her—every secret I knew. She made me feel ultra-relaxed. The emotional attachment was just welling up inside, and I didn't want to give it up.

She was stronger than I was—I admit it. I felt like I was standing on a highway with my shoes glued to the pavement, and a semi was bearing down on me. My only hope was that it would turn off the road somehow.

I saw everything I'd been working for—everything I thought God was doing in the church—about to be smashed.

Gary sent notice of his resignation, effective August 1, to the church board and the state presbyter. The presbyter called to say, "I just wanted to know if you meant what you said in your letter."

"Yes, I did," Gary replied.

"OK. Sometimes people don't, so I just wanted to check." That was all.

The prospect of the Ewings leaving for New Mexico struck fear in Rachel Fontaine. Two weeks before, she informed Gary she was pregnant. That put the final nail in the coffin of his marriage, Gary assumed; once Pam found out, she would surely evict him.

The move south proved short-lived, however; for some reason, Pastor Coffey seemed less welcoming than when they had lived there before. Gary could not find work, and so the Ewings retreated to Pam's parents farm back in Idaho. Gary persisted in trying to keep his wife and his lover in the dark about each other. Rachel raised the ante by informing him that a doctor's test had revealed the baby would be a boy, and later on, *twin* boys (Gary had four daughters). She produced an ultrasound picture of the fetuses.

The pressure was overwhelming. Gary says:

I couldn't think straight. There was no way out of this swamp. It was horrendous.

You get so deceived. I was thinking, *God, where are you?! All I wanted in life was to mind my own business and get rich. And then you put this thing in my heart about preaching, winning souls. I was just trying to help you, and now I'm losing everything. Why couldn't you give me enough strength to deal with this? Where are all the other Christians to help?*

When I think back now, I can't believe my own hypocrisy. I mean, Rachel and I would go out to a restaurant—and bow our heads together to pray over the food! Habit, I guess. And yet we were sleeping together.

Sometime after Christmas, as Rachel's demands increased, Gary finally told his wife the whole sordid story. He confessed his unfaithfulness and then asked if Pam wanted him to pack up and leave.

At first, through her sobbing, she said yes. But then, she changed her mind. A new thought struck her brain: "How do you *know* she's pregnant? Have you been to the doctor with her?"

Gary had not. Could this all be a hoax? Her weight gain *had* seemed suspiciously small to this point, even though she was a tall woman who concealed her pregnancies a long time, she said. He began asking hard questions. Within days he got to the truth: Rachel was not pregnant at all. The ultrasound had been borrowed from a nurse friend.

That angered him enough to dismiss Rachel Fontaine from his life for good.

The Ewing marriage was rebuilt slowly, gradually.

We spent six months of not doing very much at all, just living on her folks' farm. I ran a lot, baled some hay, milked cows. It was the best thing that could have happened to us.

I realized I'd never really let Pam know me. I'd kept everybody out and tried to control them.

For the first time we were understanding each other. We'd both wanted each other to be something different. Pam has always wanted to have a nice home and take care of her kids, have me go to work at eight and come home at five. And I've always wanted her to be my little queen so I could buy her nice clothes and make everybody notice her.

I have now learned to appreciate her solidness. I'm content to let her be herself.

Pam says she has gradually come to trust her husband once again. How did she survive the nearly twelve months of agony? "I don't know. A lot of the time I was in the dark, because he kept denying everything. I guess the Lord just helped me through." She is not the kind to philosophize about such matters; she simply takes life, and her mercurial husband, a day at a time.

Meanwhile, the fledgling ministry of Gary Ewing has been nearly killed. He spent two years wandering from job to job, seeking direction. Then he accepted an invitation to try to revive a dying independent congregation in rural Montana, and after sixteen months there, moved on to a similar situation fifty miles away. Rumors of his past have followed him to both locations.

He still manages to attract people to his churches; he retains that ability to light a fire, get things going. Will he make it as a pastor? If he had not been so badly handled up to now and had not made such tragic errors of his own, he might have become a useful servant for the long term. But as things stand, Gary Ewing's future is a question mark.

REFLECTIONS
by David Seamands

We get a lot of applicants like Gary Ewing here at the seminary—the older student who now thinks he should be a preacher. He was successful in a secular line of work and an energetic lay worker in the church, so his pastor nudged him our direction.

Sometimes things work out well, but in other cases, great frustration sets in. These men go suddenly from affluence to poverty, living off the equity of the nice home they sold; the wife has to go to work, the teenage children wonder what in the world is going on, and there's great disruption. Several of these cases, I am sorry to say, have ended in affairs.

Someone once asked Dwight L. Moody what was the greatest thing he had done in life. He thought awhile and finally said, "I talked ten thousand laymen out of entering the ministry." He always claimed he was just a shoe salesman himself.

When Gary Ewing was plunged into a pastorate after only one year of formal ministerial training, it is perhaps not surprising that he could not cope with a Rachel Fontaine. I find it significant that she is the daughter of a ministerial home. The chief way for religious kids to get even with their parents is to hurt them in some moral or religious sphere. By pulling down "the ministry," they achieve their goals.

The story of Gary telling his state presbyter about the situation is tragic. Here is a man who is such an institutionalist that he misses altogether the fact of a person struggling, whose whole ministry and life are at stake. He thinks only of apportionments. I am afraid this kind of blindness is not unusual among church officials. Some groups talk much about pluralism, but the application is selective: "Live like you want, believe what you want—but be sure to support the institution." I exaggerate, but not by much.

Gary Ewing does not really tell his wife the whole story, which is why she does not explode as we could have wished. He says only that he is being chased—not that it feels good to be chased.

Gary nevertheless wants *somebody* to get tough with him. He hopes Pam will scratch Rachel's eyes out, he says. As it happens, neither his presbyter nor his wife takes him seriously.

The wives I know who have saved the day have said, "Well, I understand that you're a man, and I understand your problems, but I want you to know if that happens anymore, I'm going to do such-and-such."

Gary finally resigns the church. Now, look at that perfunctory call from the presbyter. Here was the chance not for the tough line but for tender concern: "Gary, please come and see me. What's this about?" Redemption could have come at that point, still early in the adulterous relationship.

Months later, when the jig is finally up, Pam's womanly wisdom is fascinating; she nails the fake pregnancy right away! It takes one to know one, I suppose. This was the oldest trick in history, but Gary was so consumed with guilt he wasn't thinking straight. We men are so stupid sometimes—which is another reason why we should respect our wives' intuitions. They know the woman who's after us; my wife has warned me so many times, and I've said, "You're crazy! Don't be ridiculous." I'm sorry to say, she's been right every time.

She has even sometimes said, "Everybody in the church knows it but you." That's *really* embarrassing.

The incredible lengths to which people will go to maintain affairs is amazing. I remember dealing with one minister in an affair, and the amount of money he was spending to maintain it came to thousands and thousands. His family, meanwhile, was almost in poverty.

Affairs always involve lying and hypocrisy. This, however, sometimes brings people to their senses as they ask, *What in the world is happening to me? I've become a professional liar and cheater; my whole character has deteriorated.*

TWENTY-ONE

The Coffeys:
A STAFF INFECTION

The Las Cruces church to which the Ewings fled that August had risen sharply in all district standings—membership, attendance, giving—under the leadership of Bill and Ruth Coffey.

One cloud, however, was their teenage son Darin, who had been charting his own course ever since junior high. His choice of friends, his music tastes, and his insolence were but the tip of the iceberg; a school principal finally confronted Bill and Ruth with Darin's smoking, and there were hints of drugs as well.

When the boy turned sixteen—the week after police had picked him up in a friend's car that contained marijuana—Bill had decided something had to change. His reprimands had gotten nowhere, he felt; maybe if Darin sensed how close he was to adulthood, he would be more responsible. He announced a hands-off approach. Ruth Coffey, on the other hand, viewed this as capitulation. She and her husband talked often about their differing strategies but always seemed to end in stalemate.

One person who tended to see it the pastor's way was the minister of youth and music, a thirtyish single woman who had recently come to the church staff. Chris Jackson, from El Paso, held a master's degree in Christian education and was well liked by the youth group. She would take Darin out to dinner occasionally and try, in a friendly, nonauthoritarian way, to get him talking about his life. "It was obvious that here was a troubled kid," she says. "So while I felt very close to Bill and Ruth—she was almost like an older sister to me—I also tried to do what I could for Darin." The boy was wary, though, and kept the talk on a superficial level.

When office conversation would drift around to the pastor's son, Chris would volunteer her guess that Darin would learn more by natural consequence than by further parental restraints or harangues. "He's not a little boy anymore," she remembers saying, as Bill nodded. "He's almost a grown man."

One time Chris was invited to the Coffey home for dinner on a day when there had been another incident at school. "I could sense the difference between Bill's approach and Ruth's," she remembers. "Ruth was still protecting; in her mind, Bill ought to go down there and straighten things out. I just sat back thinking, *You can't do that forever. He's got to take some responsibility for his own actions.*"

When the Ewings landed back in town from Idaho, Gary updated Bill Coffey on his aborted pastorate. He said he was still being pursued by the young woman in Idaho and finally felt he needed to leave the church there. He did not mention his actual involvement with Rachel.

Bill Coffey said little in response, and in the days that followed, contact between the two men was minimal. Gary became suspicious. He watched the interaction with Chris Jackson for a while and finally went to his friend. "Something's not right here. You're spending too much time with Chris. Believe me, I know what I'm talking about!"

The seasoned pastor, now in his twenty-first year of church leadership, shook his head. "Chris and I have a very professional relationship. She does her work, and I do mine. There's nothing to worry about."

In fact, their joint concern over Darin made it difficult to discern the boundaries of professionalism. More than once they discussed the boy's latest rebellion and pondered what to do. When Darin agreed to go along with a van-full of other high schoolers that fall to see the denominational college in San Antonio, both his father and Chris were pleased. Maybe he'd wind up on a Christian campus and straighten out his life.

Chris remembers:

It was a real good trip. The kids got along great together, and even Darin seemed to open up. We stayed overnight in the dorms and had lots of fun.

But coming back from that trip, there were some little things that happened, and all of a sudden I began to feel something within myself toward Bill I'd never felt before. It was odd. In my mind, I kept thinking, *We've worked together in this church so well, and Bill would never make any kind of advance toward me. He's just not that kind of man.* I trusted him completely.

In fact, I'd been a single adult almost ten years at that point and had plenty of chances to fall in love. I was secure in my singleness; I wasn't looking for anybody.

Bill Coffey, raised in a strict environment, had been a model of propriety all through his ministry. He knew well how to rebuff temptation and preached on it often. A few days after the San Antonio trip, he and his wife were driving somewhere, and he said in a casual way, "You know how you said one time that Chris gives great back rubs? You're right. We were having a Halloween party with the kids down at the college, and my back was hurting. I just sat in a chair, and she really got the kinks out."

Ruth Coffey froze inside.

I wanted to scream, *Bill, I can't believe you did that!* But the words just locked in my throat. I'd always said I was *not* a jealous wife.

It was true that he has back trouble, and so I guess it was fine for somebody in the group to help him. But still, it scared me to death.

Six weeks later, the forty-one-year-old pastor and his minister of youth and music were in bed together.

Bill looks back at the suddenness of it all and is still perplexed at how self-control evaporated.

I was in a situation I never felt I'd be in. I'd always been able to handle any temptation up to that point.

Some people say we are intellectual beings with emotions, but I'm not so sure anymore. I'm afraid we're emotional beings with intellect instead. I keep thinking about a car analogy. Intellect is the steering wheel. It's a marvelous tool as long as all four wheels are on the road and going straight. But once you go into a skid, the steering wheel is virtually useless. When the forces of emotion take over, turning the wheel doesn't change very much.

Be that as it may, I can testify today that all the "wages of sin" I'd described in sermons came true. Loss of self-respect, fear, guilt, shame, physical deterioration, financial loss—every one of them hit.

Was Darin's waywardness the gust of wind that sent Bill Coffey into his skid? This remains a major difference of opinion. Says Ruth:

He blew that totally out of proportion because of his guilt. He had to blame somebody, and Darin caught the brunt of it. That hurts me to this day; it's not right.

I was upset about Darin, too, wasn't I? But I coped. We had always said, "We love our children for what they are, not for what we want them to be." The biggest sadness of this whole mess for me is that Darin became the scapegoat.

On the surface, nothing changed in Las Cruces for nearly a year. Bill Coffey continued to pastor the church, his attractive, dark-haired wife at his side. Chris Jackson put together another summer work trip to Mexico for the youth group. The congregation knew nothing of the inner turmoil.

Bill and Chris repeatedly vowed to stop their liaison. Too much was at stake; both of their ministries would be ruined if they did not quit. It was *over*. All such resolutions were soon broken. Says Bill:

> At first it seemed like a dream. This couldn't be happening. But the longer I went, the more conniving and covering up . . . I'd schedule more and more guest speakers or music groups for Sunday night services, just to avoid having to go into that pulpit and preach. I was just hanging on.
>
> When you get scared, you do some pretty stupid things. You're not thinking straight. Finally, Chris and I became so fearful we just packed up one Monday, took some money out of my checking account, and starting driving west toward Arizona. We had no idea where we were going. We just had to get away from the scene.
>
> Before I left, I went off by the riverbank and wrote my family a long letter. It was almost like a suicide note. I told them I loved them, and I hated what I was doing, but there was no way to change things now. I sealed the letter in an envelope and gave it to my secretary to hand-deliver to Ruth.

Ruth remembers noticing that morning, as she dressed to go to her job at a bank, that Bill had quietly observed her. She thought it unusual but was a bit flattered by the attention. Getting Bill to respond to her physically had been a pull throughout their marriage, she says; unlike most couples, "he was the one who had the headaches. I'd learned to accept what love he could give and be satisfied with it, even though I wanted more."

During the day, she called home several times; there was no answer. The last time she tried, Darin answered the phone. He said his father was not around, but his car was there, and his keys were lying on the kitchen ledge. That was strange indeed.

The church secretary was waiting for Ruth at the end of the day. "Get in the car," she said. She then handed her the fateful envelope.

I opened it, and the very first paragraph said he was sexually involved with Chris. They'd gone on a trip somewhere in Chris's car and would contact me in two weeks. In the meantime, I was to pack up his books from the church office and get ready to move.

I started screaming. Everything was just going crazy inside me. It was like I was somebody else. We went inside, and I paced the floor until I was so tired I collapsed on the couch.

When I handed the letter to Darin, he read the first paragraph and ripped it in two without going farther. He grabbed his coat and said he was going down to the river. I started screaming again. I was afraid he was going to jump in! Actually, all he wanted to do was think.

The secretary was about ready to take me to the hospital to get a shot or something when the phone rang. Darin answered, and I heard him say, "No, you don't want to talk to her." I knew it was Bill. I grabbed the phone out of my son's hand.

What had happened was that the runaway couple had stopped at a motel in Tucson, 250 miles away, and Chris had called her mother back in El Paso. A stern lecture crackled through the phone lines, and by the time Chris hung up, she had been persuaded to take a bus back to her parents' home. Bill could drive on alone. The lunacy of this escapade began to dawn on them both. Bill finally called home.

Ruth pled with him to return; if only they could talk, things could work out. Bill wanted to know if she could accept and forgive Chris. Yes, yes—anything; just come back, she urged. Bill agreed. He says:

The truth is, I was scared to death. I needed somebody to tell me what to do, and that's what Ruth did. I was a sick man. I felt like I was floating in outer space.

We drove back the next day and told Ruth it [the affair] was all over. She cried; we all cried together. Chris's parents came up and took her home for a couple of days. I made an appointment to see a doctor, who gave me an antidepressant and prescribed three weeks of rest. As far as the church was concerned, I was "ill." That's a great cover-up, you know.

Ruth and Bill spent several days away in the mountains. The next week, he announced to his wife that this was "Victory Day"—he had spent the day in prayer, and God had cleansed both body and soul. They went out to dinner to celebrate. Who was invited to share in the rejoicing? Chris Jackson.

The idea that Chris should leave Las Cruces was talked about repeatedly, but neither she nor the pastor could quite see it as necessary. They had overcome their problem, their sin had been confessed and forgiven; no need to rock the church. Besides that, she and Ruth still genuinely loved each other. Says Ruth:

> She was so talented. She was my best friend, kind of like a little sister. We went shopping together, went to exercise classes together. She'd been at our house for meals constantly, and we'd been to her place a lot, too.
>
> She even stayed with us sometimes. I made her bed—probably made *their* bed and didn't know it.

Chris, who calls herself a "survivor," showed the greatest stamina throughout this time. She alone was back at her post of duty the following Sunday, leading the youth group and directing the choir. She reflects:

> I don't know how many times I said to myself, *We're going to make it. Bill's going to get his act together, and so am I.*
>
> Throughout the whole struggle, Ruth was very compassionate and tender towards me. The longer things went on, the more time she and I spent together. It was like maybe she was trying to figure out what Bill had been attracted to. I remember she'd call me from work two or three times a day just to talk. She'd say, "I'm really full of fear, Chris. What am I going to do?" We'd pray together.

For the first time in my life, though, I realized what Romans 7 means about the struggle with sin. I was praying for Bill and Ruth to rebuild their relationship, but there was also an undercurrent of "Lord, if they can't make it work, please give me the chance to make him happy." I prayed for the Lord to take my feelings of love away, or help me meet somebody else—anything.

Good intentions notwithstanding, Bill and Chris continued to find each other irresistible. In May, at an annual district convention, Chris's mother confided to Ruth that she feared the affair was still alive. That night on the way home, Ruth told her husband what she had heard and then softly said, "It's still going on, isn't it?"

There was a long pause. Finally he said yes.

Ruth was not the longsuffering forgiver this time; she blew up. She insisted on an immediate confrontation with Chris. The three met at the church around midnight. Sharp words flew, followed by tears, and soon Bill was again promising, "Never again."

Ruth at this point began thinking of suicide. By June she laid a plan to asphyxiate herself in the garage while her husband was away the following week, and Chris was gone to youth camp. She said to Chris, "Well, when you get back, everything will be fine—you'll have exactly what you want." Chris caught the clue and demanded that Ruth do nothing until she returned; then they would have another long talk. Ruth backed down.

In July, the threesome decided to seek professional help. An appointment was made with a Christian counselor in El Paso, who was surprised to see all three of the principals in his waiting room. Says Bill:

> He was a very benevolent man, but he just didn't know how to cope with what he was seeing. Because I was a pastor, he gave me a book to read on David and Bathsheba. I read it and came back the next week with some questions.
>
> "Tell me this," I said. "Why, after the adultery, did God allow him to keep Bathsheba? And why does the lineage of Jesus, in

fact, run through her? Why didn't God make him give her up?"
He couldn't answer me. He just went on to tell me about the pain,
the physical and emotional toll I was going to have to pay. And in
that, he was exactly right. Everything he predicted came to pass.

A trip to a ministerial counseling service in Denver produced no better results. Bill was powerless to shake off the
attachment to this bright, well-educated, hard-working woman
who deeply loved him in return. His wife was willing to
forgive him even yet, he knew. But what could he say or do
now that had not already been tried?

The lid would soon blow off in the church. The secretary
had kept her mouth shut up to now, but how long could that
last? He had already used the sickness alibi to explain his
absences. There was nothing to do but resign and hope a new
pastor could be called quickly, so the congregation would not
be shattered.

Bill announced his resignation in October. He remembers,
ironically, that a special film series was underway those particular weeks: Dr. James Dobson's *Focus on the Family*. Ruth,
hopeful to the end, had tried to persuade him not to leave the
church but simply to dismiss Chris so they could rebuild. He
refused.

He lost his nerve the first Sunday he intended to read his
resignation, so he printed it in the bulletin the following week
instead. The congregation was perplexed but put together a
large fellowship dinner regardless to say farewell. By the next
Sunday, Bill had left for Albuquerque and rented an apartment, leaving his wife behind to sell the house and continue
working through Christmas, when her bank paid a year-end
bonus.

Chris Jackson hung on until the Christmas musical was
finished and then resigned as well. By New Year's Day, she
had left for Kentucky to stay with a married sister. Several
weeks before, however, Darin Coffey—the young rebel she
had originally thought to help—came to see her.

He lashed out at me and told me to please get out of his father's life. I told him I was trying to do exactly that, as soon as the Christmas musical was over. He said something like "You've all been on my case about what I've been doing and how I live. Well, at least I'm not sleeping with a married woman."

Darin and his mother went to Albuquerque after the holidays to join Bill. A concerned pastor there, a long-time friend, counseled them to maintain the form of marriage whether the feelings were present or not. Bill had by then found a job with the school district's maintenance department.

The fighting was now over. But so was the will to try once more, to hope. Sometime in March, Ruth moved out, leaving a note saying she realized she was no longer wanted. Says Bill:

> It wasn't that I didn't want her so much as the fact I just couldn't pull out of my tailspin. We were just destroying each other. A couple of months later I finally made up my mind to file for divorce. I sat in that attorney's office just whipped.
>
> The day after the divorce was granted, I loaded up my car and headed for Kentucky. Not to say that was right, but that's what happened.

A month later, he and Chris were married. They spent the next two years patching together a livelihood through a variety of jobs. Then, the chance came to manage a nursing home owned by an association of churches. They serve there today.

Ruth, meanwhile, lives with Darin in a small apartment in Albuquerque. Her son at last was brought to his senses by a serious accident at his construction job; both legs were broken by a falling beam. In the hospital, his older sister urged him to return to the faith of his childhood, and he repented. A definite change of lifestyle followed.

Ruth, the former pastor's wife, now finds herself organizing socials for the singles group she belongs to at church. She works in an office by day and cares for an elderly woman on the side in order to make ends meet. Quietly she says:

When I get depressed, I sort of pity myself, I guess. I start thinking, *There he is, married to the one he wanted, with a nice position again and everything. And here I am trying to make it alone, with no one to hold me at night—AND I DIDN'T DO ANYTHING!* In fact, I was willing to settle for so little.

I try not to let that kind of thing last, though. I just wish I'd been told in the beginning of my marriage that my husband was not a god. I loved him more than anyone in the whole wide world, and I honestly believed he could do no wrong. By the time I woke up, it was too late.

Bill Coffey does not attempt to defend his actions or blame anyone but himself for the demise of his pastoral ministry. He surrendered his credentials voluntarily. He attributes his fall to undiagnosed pride.

I had become an achiever in my church and in the state, and I was proud without knowing it. When a pastor gets to the point of thinking he's safe, and nothing can penetrate his shell, he's in danger.

Now, when I'm with a group of ministers in a restaurant, and someone flirts with the waitress, it absolutely scares me to death. If they only knew . . .

He returns at times to read what he calls "The Ex-Pastor's Psalm," the thirty-eighth, which he prayed almost daily for a while. It is, to him, a none-too-graphic description of what it is like to torpedo one's ministry through infidelity. It is a prayer of brokenness, of collapse:

O Lord, do not rebuke me in your anger
    or discipline me in your wrath. . . .
My guilt has overwhelmed me
    like a burden too heavy to bear.

My wounds fester and are loathsome
    because of my sinful folly.
I am bowed down and brought very low;
    all day long I go about mourning.

My back is filled with searing pain;
  there is no health in my body.
I am feeble and utterly crushed;
  I groan in anguish of heart.

All my longings lie open before you, O Lord:
  my sighing is not hidden from you.
My heart pounds, my strength fails me;
  even the light has gone from my eyes.
My friends and companions avoid me because of my wounds;
  my neighbors stay far away. . . .

I am like a deaf man, who cannot hear,
  like a mute, who cannot open his mouth;
I have become like a man who does not hear,
  whose mouth can offer no reply.
I wait for you, O Lord;
  you will answer, O Lord my God.
For I said, "Do not let them gloat
  or exalt themselves over me when my foot slips."

For I am about to fall,
  and my pain is ever with me.
I confess my iniquity;
  I am troubled by my sin. . . .
O Lord, do not forsake me;
  be not far from me, O my God.
Come quickly to help me,
  O Lord my Savior.

REFLECTIONS
by David Seamands

The difference between the Ewings and the Coffeys is, among
other things, a matter of timing. The Bill Coffey–Chris Jackson
affair was sustained for many months. In the end, the bonding

proved irreversible. That's what sex was created to do. They say a spider web is the strongest thing in the universe for its weight. I'd agree with that—second only to sexual bonding. The longer an affair goes on, the more two people get wrapped up with each other until they cannot be separated. It has to be broken early, as in the first two cases: either preventively by the confession, or by a shock treatment.

Neither Nick Scully nor Gary Ewing had nearly as much to lose, professionally speaking, as did Bill Coffey. His story reminded me of three of the most outstanding classmates in my graduating group who fell to sexual temptation at the top of their careers and are now out of the ministry. I sometimes wonder whether success wasn't really their god. Had they in fact made that surrender of spiritual ego that is essential for the minister? After all, one can reorganize a carnal ego around religious things. The drive to be the top jazz trumpeter or the top lawyer or the top surgeon is the same as the person who says, "I've got to be pastor of First Church, Jerusalem—not Fourth Church, Bethany." It's basically the same sin.

If such a person reaches the goal, he may feel there is nothing left to achieve. After the thrill of the chase, when you've got the fox—what else? If you're playing for the grandstand rather than the Coach, you think you need something more.

The fall isn't particularly intentional. But an unsurrendered ego will often fall at the point of sex, like David after his greatest military victory.

I realize this is a theory. But I've watched enough situations to see that a false idea of success (as Chambers said) is deadly. Ministers who have gotten their identity and fulfillment not from serving God but from using God to serve their egos are more vulnerable. After all, we are made for something even greater than First Church, Jerusalem.

The Coffey experience includes several early warnings that a missile is going to strike. Gary Ewing is one of those whom the Lord sent along, I believe. He was ignored.

Ruth, of course, should have blown a fuse over the back rub. She got angry, she was shocked—but she swallowed her words. She was not tough enough. I repeat: What right have we *not* to be jealous over our marriages? If ours is a jealous God, we should be jealous husbands and wives, in the right sense.

There is also an unsatisfactory sex life here; in this case, the husband holds back. This should have been a warning. Suddenly he discovered he was more sexually minded than he thought.

Some readers may think his comments about the human emotion and the will are self-justifying, but I find them basically accurate. The intense emotional push of an affair can hardly be described. It is a compulsion. After a certain point, the will doesn't have a chance. People will sell their souls, jobs, reputations, children, marriage—they will literally chuck *everything*. The Book of Proverbs is filled with warnings about forbidden fruit being hardest to resist. Once this toboggan starts over the hill, it is terribly hard to stop.

That's why wives ought to blow up and bishops ought to intervene right away. Outside forces are often the only way to make a man stop. He's skidding downhill; he has to be grabbed. Nothing inside the car is powerful enough.

There ought to be an extra line in Jeremiah's verse about "The heart is deceitful above all things, and desperately wicked." The further sentence should read, "The lusting heart is the most deceitful of all." Bill Coffey announces "Victory Day," the conquest of his problem, the restoration of his commitment to Ruth—and how do they celebrate? They invite Chris to dinner! Yes, this is a true story. Can you believe the self-deception?

Have you ever noticed in 2 Timothy 2 how Paul talks about enduring hardness as a good soldier? He mentions the athlete and the farmer, too—all tough jobs that call us to stand up and fight. But when it comes to lust (verse 22), he says, "Flee! Get out of there as fast as you can. Don't fool with your armor, buckle on your sword, or get your pistol ready. You don't have a chance. You're outgunned before you start." (That's the Revised Seamands Version.)

That's what Joseph did in the Old Testament. There was no way to stand and discuss things with Potiphar's wife. He *ran*.

People who have been romantically involved come to me sometimes and say, "Oh, but I still pray for him/her."

I say, "Cut it out. No more praying. Prayer is an emotional tie to that person. You're past the point of doing any good by praying."

The Phillips version of Ephesians 4:27 ("Neither give place to the devil") is this: "Don't give the devil that sort of foothold." Fantasy lust is like a beachhead from which the rest of the island is attacked. There is indeed a force of evil that lures us to unfaithfulness. It's more than human.

The longer the Coffey case goes on, the more we see Bill's difficulty in connecting truth with deed. It is as if he cannot match up what he knows with how he is acting.

Men and women in ministry together must be extremely careful and bend over absolutely backward to preserve purity. That's why Jesus taught us to pray against being led into temptation. I take that to mean, "Give me the good sense, Lord, to keep out of alluring situations, because if I get into them, I know exactly what I'm capable of doing and what I *will* do."

In place after place these last two crises could have been handled more redemptively. God might have been able to use them as shock treatments to build better marriages for both the Ewings and the Coffeys. That does not mean I endorse affairs! But I have seen the correct handling of such events give couples new foundations to build on. It shocks one spouse or the other into realizing what has been lacking and where they need to go from there.

In that sense, temptation is not unlike the other kinds of personal stresses we studied earlier. Moral breakdown does not have to cause a break*up*. It can instead become a break*through*.

TWENTY-TWO

HOLDING THIS FORT

Our reconnaisance of the weap-
onry poised against the fort of ministry marriage is now finished. Together, we have held a flashlight to as many mortars
and grenades as we could find. We have seen what they can
do in the lives of others no less worthy than ourselves.

We have also found that there is no all-purpose invention
for defense. Counseling helps sometimes, but not always.
Prayer has rescued more than one couple in trouble, but others have seemed unable to break through to God on their
knees. Planning, careful scheduling, systems: these all have
their place—and their limitations. Openness and honesty are
musts in a marriage, but not even they are the whole answer.

We are cast rather into the need for eternal vigilance, responding with variable tactics to the great variety of enemies.
Many of our foes are in fact quiet; they do not announce their
coming with the shrill whine of a missile. They work unno-
ticed as long as they can.

All of us believe the proper things about Christian marriage. We teach the biblical concepts in premarital counseling
and on couples' retreats. But when it comes to our own daily
living in the castle of marriage, our doctrine is simply a plat-

form alongside the bulwark. It elevates us into superior position. What we *do* upon the platform is still up to us.

All of the ministry couples whose experiences have been told in this book would endorse the orthodox precepts. But that did not prevent them from coming under attack.

Action based on truth is what it takes to hold the fort. The action will no doubt require all the energy we have. It will press us to our limits. It will force us to concentrate when we would rather daydream. It will require us to listen carefully when we would rather sleep.

And the times will come when we have tried our best . . . and our partner lets us down. At such moments, the advice of Elisabeth Elliot to her daughter is good to remember:

> Who is it you marry? You marry a sinner. There's nobody else to marry. That ought to be obvious enough but when you love a man as you love yours it's easy to forget. You forget it for a while, and then when something happens that ought to remind you, you find yourself wondering what's the matter, how could this happen, where did things go wrong? They went wrong back in the Garden of Eden. Settle it once for all, your husband is a son of Adam. Acceptance of him—of all of him—includes acceptance of his being a sinner. He is a fallen creature in need of the same kind of redemption all the rest of us are in need of, and liable to all the temptations which are "common to man."
>
> . . .
>
> You will find yourself disarmed utterly, and your accusing spirit transformed into loving forgiveness the moment you remember that you did, in fact, marry only a sinner, and *so did he.*[1]

Even pastors are occasional sinners. So are pastor's spouses. We are not so much the elite troops defending these barricades as we are paramilitary recruits at best, rushed into service with a minimum of training. That is why we must lean upon each other for help, study one another's mistakes, forgive the lapses, and above all cleave to the sacred commitment that binds us together, whether in war or in peace.

1. Elisabeth Elliot, *Let Me Be a Woman* (Wheaton, Ill.: Tyndale, 1976), pp. 78, 80.